The Joy of Small Wins: Celebrating Daily Achievements

Shah Rukh

Published by Shah Rukh, 2024.

While every precaution has been taken in the preparation of this book, the publisher assumes no responsibility for errors or omissions, or for damages resulting from the use of the information contained herein.

THE JOY OF SMALL WINS: CELEBRATING DAILY ACHIEVEMENTS

First edition. July 25, 2024.

Copyright © 2024 Shah Rukh.

Written by Shah Rukh.

Table of Contents

Prologue

In a world that often glorifies grand achievements and monumental success, it's easy to overlook the small victories that fill our daily lives. We are conditioned to celebrate the climactic moments—graduations, promotions, and awards—while the subtle triumphs go unnoticed. Yet, it is these small wins that truly shape our days, boost our spirits, and build the foundation for larger successes.

This book, "The Joy of Small Wins: Celebrating Daily Achievements," is a tribute to the power of these everyday victories. It is an exploration of the simple yet profound moments that bring joy, fulfillment, and a sense of accomplishment into our lives. From the pleasure of perfectly brewed coffee to the satisfaction of a completed checklist, each chapter delves into a different aspect of daily life where small wins can be found and celebrated.

The concept of celebrating small wins isn't just about recognizing minor accomplishments; it's about shifting our perspective. By focusing on these moments, we learn to appreciate the journey rather than just the destination. We start to see that each day is filled with opportunities to feel successful, happy, and content. This shift in mindset can lead to greater overall well-being, increased motivation, and a deeper sense of purpose.

In these pages, you will find stories, insights, and practical tips on how to identify and celebrate your small wins. Whether it's navigating a difficult conversation, discovering a new hobby, or simply enjoying a peaceful walk in nature, each chapter will inspire you to find joy in the everyday and recognize the significance of your achievements, no matter how small they may seem.

As you embark on this journey of celebrating daily achievements, remember that each small win is a building block of a fulfilling life. Embrace these moments, cherish them, and let them propel you forward. The joy of small wins lies in their ability to transform the ordinary into the extraordinary, one moment at a time.

Chapter 1: Finding Joy in the Morning Routine

Finding joy in the morning routine is a concept that revolves around starting the day with intentionality and a positive mindset. The morning sets the tone for the rest of the day, and by establishing a routine that is both enjoyable and fulfilling, one can cultivate a sense of joy and contentment. This practice involves not just going through the motions, but truly engaging with the activities that make up the morning, appreciating each moment, and recognizing the positive impact they have on one's overall well-being.

A key aspect of finding joy in the morning routine is the concept of mindfulness. Mindfulness involves being present and fully engaged in the current activity, without being distracted by worries about the past or future. This can be applied to even the most mundane aspects of the morning routine, such as brushing teeth, making breakfast, or getting dressed. By paying attention to the sensations, sounds, and sights associated with these activities, one can transform them from mere chores into moments of calm and reflection. For example, instead of rushing through brushing teeth, one can focus on the sensation of the toothbrush on the gums, the taste of the toothpaste, and the rhythmic motion of brushing. This simple act of mindfulness can create a sense of peace and grounding, helping to set a positive tone for the day.

Incorporating activities that bring personal joy into the morning routine is another powerful way to enhance the experience. This can vary widely from person to person, depending on individual preferences and interests. Some might find joy in a morning exercise routine, whether it's a brisk walk, a yoga session, or a workout at the gym. Physical activity not only energizes the body but also releases endorphins, which can boost mood and contribute to a sense of well-being. Others might enjoy starting their day with a creative activity, such as journaling, drawing, or playing a musical instrument. These activities can provide an outlet for self-expression and creativity, allowing one to begin the day feeling fulfilled and inspired.

The morning routine can also include practices that nourish the mind and spirit. This might involve reading a book, listening to a podcast, or engaging in meditation or prayer. Reading or listening to something uplifting or educational can provide food for thought and stimulate the mind, helping one feel more alert and engaged throughout the day. Meditation or prayer, on the other hand, can offer a moment of quiet reflection and connection, providing a sense of inner peace and grounding. These practices can be particularly valuable in cultivating a positive mindset, as they encourage gratitude, mindfulness, and a focus on the present moment.

Another important element of finding joy in the morning routine is creating an environment that is conducive to positive experiences. This might involve setting up a comfortable space for morning activities, such as a cozy reading nook, a well-organized workout area, or a peaceful spot for meditation. The environment can also be enhanced with elements that engage the senses and create a pleasant atmosphere. This might include playing soft music, lighting a scented candle, or enjoying a cup of coffee or tea. By creating a sensory-rich environment, one can enhance the overall experience of the morning routine and make it something to look forward to each day.

Time management is also a crucial factor in finding joy in the morning routine. Rushing through the morning can create stress and anxiety, which can overshadow any potential joy. By waking up a little earlier and allowing ample time for each activity, one can approach the morning with a sense of calm and ease. This might involve setting a consistent wake-up time, preparing for the day the night before, or prioritizing activities that bring the most joy and fulfillment. By managing time effectively, one can create a morning routine that feels relaxed and enjoyable, rather than hurried and stressful.

The concept of finding joy in the morning routine also involves a shift in mindset. It's about viewing the morning not as a series of tasks to be completed but as an opportunity for self-care and personal growth. This mindset shift can be fostered by setting positive intentions for the day, expressing gratitude for the simple pleasures of the morning, and celebrating small achievements. For example, taking a moment to appreciate the beauty of a sunrise, savoring a delicious breakfast, or feeling a sense of accomplishment after completing a workout can all contribute to a positive and joyful start to the day. By focusing on these small moments of joy and acknowledging their significance, one can cultivate a greater sense of appreciation and contentment.

Finding joy in the morning routine is not about perfection or adhering to a rigid schedule. It's about creating a flexible and adaptable routine that aligns with one's values, interests, and needs. Life is full of unexpected changes and challenges, and the morning routine should be able to accommodate these fluctuations. This might mean being open to trying new activities, adjusting the routine as needed, or simply allowing oneself to take a break and rest when necessary. By approaching the morning routine with a sense of curiosity and openness, one can continue to find joy and fulfillment, even as circumstances change.

Chapter 2: The Art of Perfectly Brewed Coffee

The art of perfectly brewed coffee is a fascinating and complex craft that has captivated enthusiasts around the world. It's a process that involves not only the right ingredients and equipment but also a deep understanding of the variables that affect the final product. The journey to perfect coffee begins with selecting the right beans, extends through the brewing process, and culminates in the enjoyment of the beverage. This intricate dance of science and artistry offers endless possibilities for exploration and enjoyment.

The foundation of great coffee lies in the beans. The journey starts with choosing the right beans, which is a decision influenced by several factors, including origin, variety, and roast level. Coffee beans are grown in various regions around the world, each offering distinct flavor profiles due to differences in climate, soil, and altitude. For instance, beans from Ethiopia are known for their bright and fruity notes, while those from Brazil tend to have a nutty and chocolatey flavor. The variety of the coffee plant, such as Arabica or Robusta, also plays a significant role in determining the flavor profile. Arabica beans are generally prized for their complex flavors and acidity, while Robusta beans are valued for their strong, bold taste and higher caffeine content.

The roast level of the beans is another crucial factor. Roasting transforms the green coffee beans into the aromatic, flavorful brown beans we are familiar with. The roast level can range from light to dark, each offering different flavor characteristics. Light roasts preserve more of the bean's original flavor, showcasing bright acidity and fruity or floral notes. Medium roasts strike a balance between acidity and body, often highlighting caramel and nutty flavors. Dark roasts, on the other hand, emphasize the roast flavors, resulting in a rich, bold cup with low acidity and a bittersweet finish. The choice of roast level depends on personal preference and the desired flavor profile of the coffee.

Once the beans are selected, the next step is to grind them. The grind size is a critical variable in the brewing process, as it affects the extraction of flavors from the coffee grounds. The grind size should be matched to the brewing method to ensure optimal extraction. For example, a coarse grind is suitable for methods like French press and cold brew, where the coffee grounds are in contact with water for a longer time. A medium grind is ideal for drip coffee makers and pour-over methods, while a fine grind is necessary for espresso, where the water passes through the coffee grounds quickly under high pressure. An even finer grind, almost like powder, is used for Turkish coffee. The grind size not only influences the flavor but also the texture and clarity of the coffee. A consistent grind size is essential for a balanced extraction, as uneven grinds can lead to over-extraction (bitter flavors) or under-extraction (sour flavors).

Water quality and temperature are also vital components in brewing the perfect cup of coffee. Water makes up the majority of the final cup, so its quality can significantly impact the taste. Ideally, the water should be free of impurities and have a balanced mineral content. Too many minerals can result in a flat or overly bitter coffee, while too few can make the coffee taste weak or sour. The ideal temperature for brewing coffee is typically between 195°F and 205°F (90°C to 96°C). This range allows for optimal extraction of the coffee's flavor compounds. Water that is too hot can over-extract the coffee, leading to bitterness, while water that is too cool can under-extract, resulting in a weak and underwhelming cup.

The brewing method itself is another important factor in the art of coffee making. There are numerous brewing methods, each offering a unique way to experience the flavors and aromas of coffee. The French press, for example, involves steeping coarsely ground coffee in hot water and then pressing the grounds down with a plunger. This method produces a rich, full-bodied cup with a heavy mouthfeel, as the metal filter allows the oils and fine particles to pass through. The pour-over method, on the other hand, involves pouring hot water over a bed of coffee grounds in a filter, which slowly drips into a carafe or cup. This method provides greater control over the brewing process, allowing for adjustments in water temperature, pour rate, and grind size. It typically results in a clean and bright cup with well-defined flavors.

Espresso is another popular brewing method, characterized by its strong, concentrated flavor and creamy texture. It involves forcing hot water through finely-ground coffee under high pressure, resulting in a small, intense shot of coffee with a layer of crema on top. The process of pulling a perfect espresso shot requires precision and skill, as factors like grind size, water temperature, pressure, and extraction time all need to be carefully controlled. Other methods, such as the AeroPress, siphon, and cold brew, offer further variations in flavor and mouthfeel, providing coffee enthusiasts with endless opportunities for experimentation.

The equipment used in the brewing process also plays a significant role in achieving the perfect cup of coffee. High-quality grinders, such as burr grinders, are preferred for their ability to produce a consistent grind size, which is crucial for even extraction. The brewing device itself should be chosen based on the desired brewing method, whether it's a French press, pour-over dripper, espresso machine, or another tool. Maintaining the equipment, including regular cleaning and proper storage, is essential to prevent the buildup of oils and residues that can affect the taste of the coffee.

Beyond the technical aspects, the art of perfectly brewed coffee also involves an appreciation for the sensory experience. The aroma of freshly ground coffee, the sight of the crema on an espresso shot, the sound of the coffee brewing, and the taste and texture of the final cup all contribute to the enjoyment. Tasting coffee, known as cupping, is an art in itself, involving the evaluation of the coffee's aroma, flavor, acidity, body, and finish. It requires a keen palate and an understanding of the different flavor notes and characteristics that can be present in coffee, from fruity and floral to nutty, chocolatey, and spicy.

In addition to the sensory experience, the art of coffee brewing can also be seen as a ritual that brings joy and mindfulness to daily life. The process of selecting beans, grinding them, and brewing a cup of coffee can be a calming and meditative practice, offering a moment of pause and reflection in a busy day. Sharing coffee with others can also be a social ritual, fostering connection and conversation. Whether it's enjoying a quiet cup alone in the morning, brewing coffee for friends and family, or exploring new coffee varieties and brewing techniques, the art of coffee brewing offers endless opportunities for exploration and enjoyment.

Ultimately, the art of perfectly brewed coffee is a deeply personal and subjective experience. What constitutes the perfect cup of coffee can vary greatly from person to person, depending on individual preferences and tastes. Some may prefer a bold, dark roast with a strong, robust flavor, while others may enjoy a light, fruity coffee with bright acidity. The journey to discovering one's ideal coffee involves exploring different beans, roast levels, grind sizes, brewing methods, and techniques, as well as being open to trying new and unfamiliar flavors. It's a journey that can be both enriching and enjoyable, offering a deeper appreciation for the craft and artistry of coffee.

Chapter 3: Mastering the Daily Commute

Mastering the daily commute is an essential aspect of modern life for many people, especially those living in urban areas. The daily commute can significantly influence one's overall well-being, productivity, and even mental health. While commuting can sometimes be a source of stress and frustration, mastering it involves adopting strategies and habits that transform it into a more efficient, enjoyable, and productive experience. This comprehensive approach encompasses everything from choosing the right mode of transportation to optimizing time and finding ways to enhance the experience.

One of the first steps in mastering the daily commute is choosing the most suitable mode of transportation. This decision is influenced by various factors, including distance, cost, convenience, environmental impact, and personal preferences. For many, driving a car is the most convenient option, offering flexibility and privacy. However, it also comes with challenges such as traffic congestion, parking issues, and the environmental impact of emissions. To mitigate these, some commuters opt for carpooling, which reduces the number of vehicles on the road and can also make the journey more social and cost-effective. Carpooling apps and platforms have made it easier to find and coordinate with fellow commuters, further streamlining this option.

Public transportation, including buses, trains, and subways, is another common choice, especially in cities with well-developed transit systems. Public transport can be more economical and environmentally friendly compared to driving. It also allows commuters to use travel time for other activities, such as reading, working, or simply relaxing. However, the convenience of public transportation can vary greatly depending on factors like schedule reliability, overcrowding, and the availability of routes. Mastering the use of public transit involves being familiar with schedules, routes, and potential alternatives in case of delays or disruptions. Using apps and online resources to track real-time schedules and updates can significantly enhance the commuting experience, making it more predictable and less stressful.

For those who live relatively close to their workplace, biking or walking can be excellent commuting options. These modes of transport offer numerous benefits, including physical exercise, cost savings, and a smaller environmental footprint. Biking, in particular, can be faster than driving or public transport in congested areas, and many cities are increasingly investing in bike lanes and other infrastructure to support cyclists. For safety and convenience, cyclists should be equipped with proper gear, including helmets, lights, and reflective clothing, and should be aware of local traffic laws and bike routes. Walking, while generally slower, can be a refreshing and relaxing way to start and end the day, providing time for contemplation and a connection with the surroundings.

Once the mode of transportation is chosen, optimizing the commute itself is crucial. This involves planning and preparation to ensure a smooth and efficient journey. For drivers, this might mean checking traffic conditions and planning the best route in advance, using GPS and navigation apps to avoid congested areas. Leaving at the right time can also make a significant difference; starting the commute a bit earlier or later than usual rush hours can help avoid the worst traffic. For public transport users, optimizing the commute might involve choosing the best times to travel, selecting the fastest routes, and being aware of any service changes or disruptions.

Another important aspect of mastering the daily commute is making productive use of the time spent traveling. This can transform what might otherwise be seen as wasted time into an opportunity for personal growth, relaxation, or preparation for the day ahead. For those who commute by public transport or as passengers in a carpool, this might involve listening to audiobooks, podcasts, or music, which can be both entertaining and educational. Many people use this time to catch up on reading, whether for leisure or professional development, or to respond to emails and plan their day. With the increasing availability of mobile technology and internet access, the possibilities for productive activities during the commute are expanding.

For drivers, who need to focus on the road, using the commute for productive activities might involve hands-free options like audiobooks or educational podcasts. It's also a good time to engage in reflective thinking or practice mindfulness, focusing on the present moment and staying calm amidst traffic. This can help reduce stress and set a positive tone for the day. Some people find it helpful to use the commute as a time for setting goals, reviewing tasks, and mentally preparing for the day or unwinding and decompressing after work.

Creating a comfortable and pleasant environment can also enhance the commuting experience. This might include personalizing the space within a car with comfortable seating, good music, or even aromatherapy. For those using public transportation, carrying a comfortable bag, wearing appropriate clothing for the weather, and having access to snacks or water can make the journey more pleasant. Additionally, being prepared for unexpected delays or changes in plans, such as carrying a book, a fully charged phone, or a portable charger, can help alleviate frustration and boredom.

Another strategy for mastering the daily commute is incorporating physical activity into the routine. For example, parking further from the destination or getting off public transport a stop early can provide an opportunity for a brisk walk. This not only adds exercise to the day but can also be invigorating and mood-enhancing. Similarly, those who bike to work incorporate physical activity naturally into their day, which can have significant health benefits, including improved cardiovascular health and reduced stress levels.

The psychological aspect of commuting should not be overlooked. A positive mindset can significantly influence the perception of the commute. Viewing it as an opportunity rather than a chore can transform the experience. For example, the commute can be seen as a transition period that helps to separate work from home life, providing a buffer to unwind and shift gears mentally. This perspective can be particularly beneficial for those who find it challenging to switch off from work-related thoughts. Practicing gratitude, focusing on the positive aspects of the journey, and maintaining a sense of curiosity and openness can also enhance the experience.

Finally, it's important to recognize that commuting habits and preferences can change over time. What works best for an individual at one stage of life might not be ideal later on. For example, changes in job location, family responsibilities, or health can necessitate adjustments to commuting strategies. Regularly evaluating the commute and being open to trying new modes of transportation, routes, or schedules can lead to a more satisfying and efficient experience. Flexibility and adaptability are key, as is the willingness to explore new technologies and services that can make commuting more convenient and enjoyable.

Chapter 4: Conquering the First Task of the Day

Conquering the first task of the day is a fundamental strategy for setting a positive and productive tone for the hours that follow. The first task, often referred to as the "most important task" (MIT), can significantly influence one's momentum, motivation, and mindset throughout the day. Successfully tackling this initial challenge not only provides a sense of accomplishment but also creates a psychological boost that can carry over into subsequent tasks. This concept, rooted in various productivity methodologies, emphasizes the importance of prioritization, focus, and effective time management. To conquer the first task of the day, one must consider several key factors, including preparation, mindset, environment, and strategies for overcoming common obstacles.

Preparation for the first task of the day often begins the night before. By identifying the most important task ahead of time, one can start the day with clarity and purpose. This preparation involves not only deciding what task to prioritize but also gathering any necessary materials, setting up the workspace, and ensuring that all tools and resources are readily available. This reduces the likelihood of procrastination and allows for a seamless transition into the workday. For example, if the first task involves writing a report, preparation might include organizing notes, drafting an outline, and ensuring that the necessary software is up to date. By laying this groundwork, one can start the task immediately upon waking, without unnecessary delays or distractions.

The importance of selecting the right task cannot be overstated. The first task should ideally be one that has significant impact or value, either in terms of long-term goals or immediate priorities. This task is often challenging or requires a high level of focus, making it a priority to tackle when energy levels and cognitive resources are at their peak. Known as "eating the frog," this approach suggests handling the most challenging or least pleasant task first, thereby eliminating the potential for procrastination and the mental burden of dreading the task throughout the day. The sense of relief and accomplishment from completing this task can create a positive feedback loop, making it easier to maintain momentum and tackle subsequent tasks.

Mindset plays a crucial role in conquering the first task of the day. A positive, proactive mindset can enhance motivation and resilience, helping to overcome any initial resistance or reluctance. This mindset can be cultivated through various practices, such as setting clear goals, visualizing success, and affirming one's capabilities. Starting the day with a brief period of mindfulness or meditation can also help center the mind and focus on the task at hand. This practice can reduce stress and anxiety, promoting a calm and clear-headed approach to the day's challenges. Additionally, reframing the task as an opportunity rather than a chore can transform the experience, making it more enjoyable and engaging.

The physical environment in which the first task is tackled can also have a significant impact on productivity and focus. Creating a conducive workspace involves minimizing distractions, ensuring comfort, and organizing the space to support the task at hand. This might include having a clean and clutter-free desk, comfortable seating, good lighting, and easy access to all necessary tools and resources. For those working from home, it can be helpful to designate a specific area for work, separate from spaces used for relaxation or leisure. This physical separation can help signal to the brain that it's time to focus, thereby enhancing concentration and efficiency.

In addition to setting up a conducive physical environment, managing digital distractions is equally important. This might involve turning off notifications, setting devices to "Do Not Disturb," and using apps or software that block access to distracting websites or social media during work hours. By creating a digital environment that supports focus, one can reduce the temptation to multitask or get sidetracked, thereby maintaining a steady and productive workflow. Some people find it helpful to use techniques like the Pomodoro Technique, which involves working in focused bursts followed by short breaks. This approach can help maintain concentration while also preventing burnout and fatigue.

Overcoming procrastination is often a key challenge in conquering the first task of the day. Procrastination can arise from various sources, including fear of failure, perfectionism, lack of clarity, or simply a lack of motivation. To address these issues, it's helpful to break down the task into smaller, more manageable steps. This can make the task feel less overwhelming and provide a clear starting point. For example, instead of thinking about writing an entire report, one might focus on drafting just the introduction or outlining the main points. This approach, known as chunking, can make the task feel more achievable and can provide a sense of progress with each completed step.

Another effective strategy for overcoming procrastination is to set specific, measurable goals and deadlines. Having a clear deadline creates a sense of urgency, which can motivate action and prevent tasks from being indefinitely postponed. Additionally, setting specific goals for what needs to be accomplished within a certain timeframe can provide direction and focus. For instance, instead of a vague goal like "work on the project," a more specific goal might be "complete the first draft of the project proposal by noon." This specificity not only clarifies what needs to be done but also provides a benchmark for measuring progress.

Accountability can also play a significant role in conquering the first task of the day. Sharing goals and progress with a colleague, friend, or mentor can provide external motivation and support. Knowing that someone else is aware of one's goals and is expecting updates can encourage follow-through and reduce the temptation to procrastinate.

In some cases, simply verbalizing the commitment to another person can solidify the intention and increase the likelihood of taking action. For those working in teams, regular check-ins or progress meetings can provide a structured way to maintain accountability and ensure that tasks are being completed in a timely manner.

In addition to these strategies, it's important to recognize and celebrate small wins and accomplishments. Completing the first task of the day, no matter how small, is a significant achievement and deserves acknowledgment. Celebrating these victories can boost morale and reinforce positive behavior, making it more likely that the practice will continue. This celebration can take many forms, from a simple mental acknowledgment to a more tangible reward, such as taking a break, enjoying a favorite snack, or engaging in a leisure activity. By associating the completion of tasks with positive reinforcement, one can create a more enjoyable and rewarding work experience.

Finally, flexibility and adaptability are essential qualities in mastering the first task of the day. While planning and preparation are crucial, it's also important to remain flexible and adaptable in the face of unexpected changes or challenges. This might involve adjusting priorities, revising goals, or finding alternative solutions when obstacles arise. A flexible mindset allows one to navigate these challenges with resilience and creativity, rather than becoming discouraged or stuck. Embracing a growth mindset, which views challenges as opportunities for learning and growth, can further enhance one's ability to adapt and succeed.

Chapter 5: The Power of a Clean Desk

The power of a clean desk extends far beyond aesthetics; it is a fundamental aspect of productivity, mental clarity, and overall well-being. A clean desk is not just about tidiness; it represents an organized mind, a sense of control, and a readiness to tackle tasks efficiently. In the modern work environment, where distractions are abundant and workloads are often heavy, maintaining a clean desk can be a powerful tool in enhancing focus, reducing stress, and promoting a positive work atmosphere. The concept of a clean desk encompasses both the physical and digital spaces where work is conducted, and mastering it involves understanding its benefits, implementing effective organizational strategies, and maintaining a consistent routine.

One of the primary benefits of a clean desk is the enhancement of focus and concentration. A cluttered workspace can be visually distracting, drawing the eye to various unrelated items and creating a sense of chaos. This visual noise can disrupt concentration and make it difficult to prioritize tasks. In contrast, a clean desk provides a clear and organized space, free from unnecessary items that could divert attention. This simplicity allows the mind to focus more easily on the task at hand, promoting deeper concentration and reducing the likelihood of being sidetracked by irrelevant stimuli. The concept of "visual decluttering" plays a significant role here; by minimizing the number of items in the field of view, one can reduce cognitive overload and create a more serene and focused work environment.

A clean desk also fosters a sense of control and organization. In a busy work environment, where multiple projects and tasks are often competing for attention, having an organized workspace can provide a sense of order and control. This organization is not just about neatness; it involves having a designated place for everything and ensuring that only the necessary tools and materials are readily accessible. This approach can help streamline workflows, reduce the time spent searching for items, and make it easier to transition between tasks. For example, keeping frequently used documents, stationery, and digital devices within easy reach can facilitate a smoother workflow and reduce interruptions caused by searching for misplaced items.

Another significant benefit of a clean desk is the reduction of stress and anxiety. Clutter can be a constant, low-level stressor, creating a sense of overwhelm and contributing to a chaotic work environment. This clutter-related stress can be both physical and psychological. Physically, it can make it difficult to find needed items, leading to frustration and wasted time. Psychologically, clutter can serve as a constant reminder of unfinished tasks or disorganization, which can contribute to feelings of anxiety and guilt. A clean desk, on the other hand, can create a calm and peaceful environment, which can help reduce stress and promote a positive mindset. This calming effect can be particularly beneficial during busy periods or when working on complex projects that require deep focus and concentration.

In addition to these psychological benefits, a clean desk can also have practical advantages. It can improve efficiency by making it easier to locate important documents and tools, thereby reducing the time spent searching for items. This efficiency can be particularly important in time-sensitive situations, where delays caused by disorganization can have significant consequences. Furthermore, a clean desk can improve the quality of work by reducing errors that can occur when important items are misplaced or overlooked. For example, having an organized filing system can ensure that important documents are easily accessible and that deadlines are not missed.

Maintaining a clean desk also has implications for professionalism and perception, especially in shared or open office environments. A cluttered desk can give the impression of disorganization or lack of attention to detail, which can impact how colleagues, clients, or supervisors perceive an individual's work habits and reliability. In contrast, a clean and organized desk can convey a sense of professionalism, competence, and respect for the work environment. This positive perception can enhance one's reputation and credibility in the workplace, contributing to career advancement and professional relationships.

The concept of a clean desk extends beyond the physical workspace to include the digital environment. In today's digital age, much of the work is conducted on computers, and the state of one's digital workspace can be just as important as the physical one. A cluttered digital desktop, with numerous icons, open tabs, and disorganized files, can create the same sense of chaos and distraction as a cluttered physical desk. Organizing the digital workspace involves creating a logical folder structure, regularly deleting or archiving unnecessary files, and keeping the desktop clean and uncluttered. Additionally, managing email inboxes and digital tools efficiently can prevent information overload and ensure that important communications and tasks are not overlooked.

Implementing and maintaining a clean desk requires consistent effort and discipline. One effective strategy is the practice of "end-of-day tidying," where the last few minutes of the workday are dedicated to organizing the workspace. This can involve filing away papers, organizing desk items, and tidying up the digital desktop. By doing this daily, one can prevent clutter from accumulating and start the next day with a clean and organized workspace. Another helpful practice is the "one-touch rule," which involves handling each item only once. For example, when picking up a document, one decides immediately whether to file it, act on it, or discard it, rather than setting it aside to deal with later. This approach can reduce procrastination and prevent clutter from building up.

Setting boundaries and creating designated spaces for specific tasks can also help maintain a clean desk. For example, one might designate a specific area of the desk for paperwork, another for digital devices, and another for personal items. This organization can help keep different types of tasks separate and prevent items from becoming mixed and disorganized. Additionally, setting boundaries regarding what items are allowed on the desk can help maintain focus and prevent unnecessary clutter. For example, one might decide to keep only essential items on the desk and store less frequently used items in drawers or cabinets.

In addition to these organizational strategies, it's important to regularly evaluate and update the workspace to ensure it continues to meet one's needs. This might involve reassessing the organization system, decluttering, and making adjustments to improve efficiency and comfort. For example, as work responsibilities and projects change, the tools and materials needed may also change, requiring updates to the workspace setup. Regularly reassessing the workspace can help ensure it remains functional and conducive to productivity.

It's also worth noting that the benefits of a clean desk can extend beyond the individual to impact the broader work environment. In shared workspaces, maintaining a clean desk can contribute to a more pleasant and efficient work environment for everyone. It can reduce the spread of germs and create a more professional and welcoming atmosphere. Additionally, in open office environments, where visual clutter can be more noticeable and distracting, maintaining a clean desk can help create a more harmonious and focused work environment.

Chapter 6: Small Acts of Kindness

Small acts of kindness are simple, often spontaneous actions that reflect a genuine concern for the well-being of others. These gestures can range from a friendly smile to helping a stranger in need, offering words of encouragement, or simply listening attentively. While they may seem minor or inconsequential, small acts of kindness hold immense power in shaping relationships, communities, and even broader societal norms. The beauty of these acts lies in their accessibility; anyone, regardless of their resources or status, can perform them. They are not bound by grand gestures or significant financial contributions but are instead rooted in everyday interactions and the basic human capacity for empathy and compassion.

One of the most profound aspects of small acts of kindness is their impact on human connections. In a world that often feels fragmented and impersonal, these simple gestures can bridge gaps between individuals, fostering a sense of community and mutual respect. For example, a warm greeting or a friendly conversation with a neighbor can transform an otherwise mundane interaction into a meaningful connection. Such acts break down barriers, allowing people to see each other as individuals rather than strangers. This humanizes our interactions and creates a sense of belonging and shared humanity. In the workplace, small acts of kindness, such as offering to help a colleague with a task or acknowledging someone's hard work, can build camaraderie and strengthen team dynamics.

The ripple effect of small acts of kindness is another remarkable aspect of their power. When someone experiences kindness, they are often inspired to pass it on, creating a chain reaction that can extend far beyond the initial act. This phenomenon, known as the "pay it forward" effect, demonstrates how a single act of kindness can multiply and impact numerous people. For instance, a person who receives help from a stranger during a difficult moment might feel encouraged to help others in return, spreading positivity and kindness throughout their community. This ripple effect can lead to a more compassionate society, where people are more attuned to the needs of others and more willing to extend a helping hand.

Small acts of kindness also have significant psychological benefits for both the giver and the receiver. For the giver, performing acts of kindness can enhance well-being and reduce stress. The act of giving, whether it be time, resources, or emotional support, triggers the release of endorphins, the body's natural mood elevators. This phenomenon, often referred to as the "helper's high," can lead to increased feelings of happiness and satisfaction. Moreover, engaging in acts of kindness can boost self-esteem and create a sense of purpose and fulfillment, as individuals feel they are making a positive difference in the lives of others.

For the receiver, acts of kindness can provide comfort, support, and validation. In moments of hardship or loneliness, a small act of kindness can be a powerful reminder that they are not alone and that others care about their well-being. This can alleviate feelings of isolation and boost resilience, helping individuals cope with challenges more effectively. For example, receiving a handwritten note of encouragement or a thoughtful gesture during a tough time can uplift someone's spirits and provide much-needed emotional support. In this way, acts of kindness can have a profound impact on mental health, fostering a sense of connection and hope.

The practice of kindness can also transform environments, making them more welcoming and inclusive. In schools, for example, promoting small acts of kindness among students can create a more positive and supportive atmosphere. Acts such as sharing, helping peers, or simply being kind and respectful can reduce bullying and promote a culture of empathy and understanding. Similarly, in workplaces, encouraging acts of kindness can enhance the overall work culture, leading to increased employee satisfaction and productivity.

When kindness is valued and practiced regularly, it can foster an environment where individuals feel valued, respected, and motivated to contribute positively.

Furthermore, small acts of kindness can challenge and change societal norms and behaviors. In a world where competition and self-interest often dominate, kindness can be a radical act that challenges these norms. It encourages people to look beyond themselves and consider the needs and feelings of others. This shift in perspective can lead to greater empathy and a more collaborative approach to solving problems. For example, community initiatives that encourage acts of kindness, such as neighborhood clean-ups or food drives, can bring people together to address common challenges and improve the quality of life for everyone.

The accessibility of small acts of kindness makes them a powerful tool for social change. Unlike large-scale charitable donations or organized volunteer efforts, which may require significant resources or time, small acts of kindness can be performed by anyone, anywhere, at any time. They do not require extensive planning or resources, making them an inclusive and egalitarian way to make a positive impact. This accessibility means that everyone has the opportunity to contribute to a kinder, more compassionate world, regardless of their circumstances.

Another important aspect of small acts of kindness is their role in fostering gratitude. Both the giver and the receiver of kindness can experience a heightened sense of gratitude. The giver often feels grateful for the opportunity to help others and for the positive feelings that arise from the act. The receiver, on the other hand, may feel grateful for the kindness shown to them and more likely to appreciate the good things in their life. This mutual gratitude can enhance relationships and create a positive feedback loop, where acts of kindness lead to increased feelings of gratitude and a greater propensity to continue engaging in kind behaviors.

In addition to individual benefits, small acts of kindness can have economic and societal benefits. For example, simple acts such as recycling, reducing waste, or supporting local businesses can contribute to environmental sustainability and economic resilience. Kindness in consumer behavior, such as choosing ethical products or supporting businesses that give back to the community, can drive positive social and environmental change. Similarly, kindness in public services, such as healthcare and education, can improve service quality and outcomes, as individuals feel more cared for and supported.

In the context of global challenges, small acts of kindness can play a crucial role in fostering international understanding and cooperation. Acts of kindness towards people from different cultures, backgrounds, or nations can help break down stereotypes and prejudices, promoting peace and mutual respect. In times of crisis, such as natural disasters or pandemics, small acts of kindness, such as donating to relief efforts or supporting affected communities, can make a significant difference in alleviating suffering and rebuilding lives.

It is also important to recognize that small acts of kindness are not just about grand gestures or visible actions. They can be as simple as being patient in a long line, offering a smile to a stranger, or being a good listener. These seemingly minor actions can have a significant impact on someone's day and contribute to a culture of kindness and respect. Moreover, practicing kindness can lead to personal growth, as it encourages individuals to develop qualities such as empathy, patience, and understanding.

Chapter 7: Navigating Difficult Conversations

Navigating difficult conversations is a crucial skill in both personal and professional contexts, as these interactions often involve sensitive topics, strong emotions, or conflicting interests. Such conversations might include discussing workplace performance issues, addressing personal conflicts, delivering bad news, or negotiating important matters. The ability to handle these discussions effectively can prevent misunderstandings, reduce tension, and foster better relationships. It involves a combination of preparation, emotional intelligence, communication skills, and empathy. The goal is not just to resolve the issue at hand, but to do so in a way that maintains or even strengthens the relationship between the parties involved.

Preparation is a key component of navigating difficult conversations. Before entering the conversation, it's important to clarify your objectives and desired outcomes. This involves understanding not just what you want to communicate, but also what you hope to achieve. For example, if the conversation is about addressing a colleague's performance, the goal might be not just to highlight areas of improvement, but also to support their professional development and growth. Clarifying your goals helps to keep the conversation focused and ensures that it is productive. Additionally, it's helpful to anticipate the other person's perspective and possible reactions. This means considering how they might feel about the topic and what concerns or objections they might have. By preparing for these reactions, you can think about how to address them in a constructive manner.

Another crucial aspect of preparation is gathering relevant information and evidence. In situations where facts are crucial, such as in a workplace performance review or a discussion about responsibilities, it's important to have specific examples and data to support your points. This helps to ground the conversation in reality and avoids the pitfalls of subjective or vague statements, which can lead to misunderstandings or defensiveness. For instance, instead of saying, "You never meet your deadlines," providing specific instances where deadlines were missed, along with any relevant context, can make the feedback more constructive and actionable.

Emotional intelligence plays a vital role in navigating difficult conversations. This involves being aware of your own emotions and those of the other person, and managing them in a way that promotes understanding and cooperation. Recognizing and acknowledging your own emotions, such as anxiety, frustration, or anger, can help you approach the conversation more calmly and rationally. It's also important to be attuned to the other person's emotional state. Non-verbal cues such as body language, tone of voice, and facial expressions can provide valuable insights into how they are feeling. Being empathetic and showing that you understand their emotions can help to build trust and rapport, making the conversation more productive.

Effective communication skills are essential for navigating difficult conversations. This includes not only what you say but also how you say it. Clarity and directness are important; vague or ambiguous statements can lead to confusion and misinterpretation. It's helpful to use "I" statements, which focus on your own experiences and feelings rather than attributing blame or making accusations. For example, saying "I feel concerned when deadlines are missed because it affects the team's productivity" is more constructive than saying "You always miss deadlines." This approach reduces the likelihood of the other person becoming defensive and fosters a more open and honest dialogue.

Active listening is another crucial communication skill in difficult conversations. This involves fully focusing on the speaker, understanding their message, and responding thoughtfully. It's important to listen not just to the words being said, but also to the underlying emotions and concerns. Reflective listening, which involves paraphrasing what the other person has said and reflecting it back to them, can help to ensure that you have understood their perspective correctly. For example, you might say, "It sounds like you feel frustrated about the workload and are concerned that it's affecting your performance." This shows that you are engaged in the conversation and that you value the other person's perspective.

Empathy is a fundamental component of navigating difficult conversations. This involves putting yourself in the other person's shoes and trying to understand their feelings and perspective. Empathy can help to defuse tension and create a more collaborative atmosphere. It's important to acknowledge the other person's feelings and show that you understand their perspective, even if you don't agree with it. This can be as simple as saying, "I understand that this situation is difficult for you, and I appreciate your willingness to discuss it." Empathy can also involve being flexible and willing to compromise, finding solutions that address both your needs and those of the other person.

Managing emotions is a critical skill in difficult conversations. Strong emotions can cloud judgment and escalate conflict, so it's important to remain calm and composed. This doesn't mean suppressing your emotions, but rather managing them in a way that allows for constructive communication. If you find yourself becoming emotional, it can be helpful to take a deep breath, pause, and refocus on the goals of the conversation. It's also important to recognize when the other person is becoming emotional and to respond with empathy and understanding. Sometimes, taking a break or suggesting a follow-up conversation can be a good strategy if emotions are running high and productive communication is difficult.

One common challenge in difficult conversations is dealing with defensiveness. When people feel attacked or criticized, they may become defensive, which can hinder open communication and problem-solving. To minimize defensiveness, it's important to frame the conversation in a way that emphasizes mutual goals and collaboration. This might involve focusing on shared objectives, such as improving team performance or finding a solution to a problem. It's also helpful to avoid blaming language and instead focus on behaviors and actions rather than personal characteristics. For example, rather than saying "You're unreliable," you might say "I've noticed that there have been some missed deadlines, and I'd like to discuss how we can address this."

Another key aspect of navigating difficult conversations is being open to feedback and willing to listen to the other person's perspective. This means being prepared to hear things that you may not want to hear and being willing to consider their viewpoint. It's important to approach the conversation with an open mind and a willingness to learn and grow. This can involve asking open-ended questions to encourage the other person to share their thoughts and feelings. For example, you might ask, "Can you tell me more about how you see this situation?" or "What do you think we could do differently?" Being open to feedback also means being willing to acknowledge your own mistakes and take responsibility for them. This can demonstrate humility and build trust, making it easier to find a resolution.

Finally, it's important to focus on finding solutions and moving forward. The goal of a difficult conversation should not just be to air grievances or express frustrations but to find constructive ways to address the issues and improve the situation. This involves being proactive and solution-focused, brainstorming potential solutions together, and agreeing on specific actions to take. It's important to be realistic and practical in setting goals and to establish clear expectations and timelines. It can also be helpful to agree on a plan for follow-up, to ensure that the agreed-upon actions are implemented and to discuss any ongoing issues or concerns.

Chapter 8: Celebrating Healthy Choices

Celebrating healthy choices is an essential aspect of fostering a positive lifestyle and reinforcing behaviors that contribute to overall well-being. These choices encompass a wide range of actions, including healthy eating, regular physical activity, adequate sleep, stress management, and the avoidance of harmful habits like smoking or excessive alcohol consumption. By celebrating these choices, individuals and communities can cultivate a supportive environment that encourages continued commitment to health and wellness. This celebration not only serves to recognize achievements but also motivates ongoing efforts and helps to establish long-term, sustainable habits.

At the core of celebrating healthy choices is the recognition of personal milestones and achievements. This recognition can take many forms, from acknowledging small daily accomplishments to celebrating significant lifestyle changes. For example, someone who decides to incorporate more fruits and vegetables into their diet might start by adding a salad to their lunch each day. Recognizing and celebrating this small but important change can reinforce the behavior, making it more likely to become a permanent part of their routine. Over time, these small steps accumulate, leading to more substantial changes in overall diet and health. Celebrating these milestones can be as simple as a personal acknowledgment, a congratulatory note from a friend, or even a small reward, like a new book or a special outing.

The celebration of healthy choices also involves creating a positive and supportive environment. This environment can be cultivated at home, in the workplace, or within the broader community. For instance, families can celebrate healthy choices by cooking nutritious meals together, participating in physical activities, or setting shared health goals. In the workplace, employers can support healthy choices by offering wellness programs, providing healthy snacks, or organizing group fitness activities. Communities can celebrate healthy living through events like farmers' markets, health fairs, or public fitness challenges. These environments provide the social support and encouragement needed to maintain healthy behaviors and can be a source of inspiration and motivation for others.

An important aspect of celebrating healthy choices is the focus on positive reinforcement rather than punitive measures. Positive reinforcement involves acknowledging and rewarding healthy behaviors, which can encourage individuals to continue making good choices. This approach is often more effective than focusing solely on the negative consequences of unhealthy behaviors. For example, rather than emphasizing the risks associated with a sedentary lifestyle, celebrating the benefits of regular physical activity—such as improved mood, increased energy, and better sleep—can be more motivating. Positive reinforcement can also include recognizing the effort and determination involved in making healthy changes, even if the results are not immediately apparent.

The celebration of healthy choices is not limited to individual actions; it also encompasses the promotion of a broader culture of health and wellness. This culture can be fostered through public health campaigns, education, and policies that support healthy living. For example, public health initiatives that encourage regular physical activity, balanced nutrition, and preventive healthcare can help create a societal norm that values health and wellness. Education plays a crucial role in this process, as it provides individuals with the knowledge and skills needed to make informed choices. Policies, such as those that promote smoke-free environments, access to nutritious food, and safe spaces for physical activity, can further support a culture of health by making healthy choices more accessible and convenient.

The celebration of healthy choices also involves addressing and overcoming barriers that may prevent individuals from making these choices. These barriers can include lack of access to healthy food, safe places for exercise, healthcare, and education about health and wellness. Celebrating healthy choices includes advocating for policies and programs that address these barriers and promote health equity. For example, initiatives that provide affordable fresh produce in food deserts, create safe walking and biking paths, or offer free health screenings can help ensure that everyone has the opportunity to make healthy choices. By addressing these systemic issues, communities can create an environment where healthy living is accessible to all, regardless of socioeconomic status or geographic location.

In addition to physical health, celebrating healthy choices also involves recognizing and promoting mental and emotional well-being. This includes practices such as mindfulness, stress management, and seeking support when needed. Celebrating these aspects of health can involve acknowledging the importance of taking time for self-care, setting boundaries, and finding healthy ways to cope with stress. For example, someone who makes the choice to meditate regularly, seek therapy, or practice gratitude can be celebrated for prioritizing their mental health. This recognition helps to reduce the stigma associated with mental health issues and encourages a more holistic approach to well-being.

Another important element of celebrating healthy choices is the emphasis on sustainability and long-term change. Making healthy choices is not about temporary diets or quick fixes; it involves adopting habits and behaviors that can be sustained over the long term. This includes setting realistic and achievable goals, being patient with oneself, and recognizing that setbacks are a natural part of the process. Celebrating healthy choices involves recognizing progress rather than perfection and understanding that every step towards a healthier lifestyle is valuable. This approach helps to build resilience and persistence, which are crucial for maintaining healthy behaviors over time.

The celebration of healthy choices also includes the sharing of knowledge and experiences. This can involve sharing recipes, workout routines, stress-relief techniques, or personal stories of transformation. By sharing these experiences, individuals can inspire and motivate others, creating a ripple effect of positive change. This sharing can occur through social media, community groups, or informal conversations. Celebrating healthy choices together can create a sense of community and shared purpose, which can be incredibly motivating and empowering. It also provides an opportunity for individuals to learn from each other and discover new ways to incorporate healthy choices into their lives.

Moreover, celebrating healthy choices can have a significant impact on the next generation. When children see adults making and celebrating healthy choices, they are more likely to adopt these behaviors themselves. This can be particularly impactful in areas such as nutrition, physical activity, and mental health. For example, parents who involve their children in cooking healthy meals or participate in family physical activities are teaching valuable skills and habits that can last a lifetime. Schools and community programs that celebrate and promote healthy choices can also play a crucial role in shaping the habits and attitudes of young people.

Chapter 9: Embracing New Learning Opportunities

Embracing new learning opportunities is a vital aspect of personal and professional growth, fostering continuous development and adaptation in a rapidly changing world. The process involves a proactive attitude towards acquiring new skills, knowledge, and experiences, which can lead to greater self-awareness, improved capabilities, and expanded perspectives. In an era characterized by technological advancements, globalization, and evolving industries, the ability to embrace new learning opportunities is not just beneficial but essential for staying relevant and competitive.

At its core, embracing new learning opportunities requires an open and curious mindset. This means being willing to step out of one's comfort zone and explore unfamiliar areas. It involves recognizing that learning is a lifelong process and that there is always something new to discover, regardless of one's age, profession, or level of expertise. This mindset is often characterized by a thirst for knowledge, a willingness to ask questions, and a readiness to seek out new experiences. For example, an individual might take up a new hobby, enroll in a course, attend workshops or seminars, or even travel to new places. Each of these experiences offers unique learning opportunities that can broaden one's horizons and enhance one's understanding of the world.

One significant aspect of embracing new learning opportunities is the recognition of the diverse forms of learning available. Learning is not confined to traditional educational settings like schools and universities; it can take place in various environments and through different mediums. Formal education, such as degree programs and certifications, provides structured learning with clear objectives and outcomes. Informal learning, on the other hand, includes experiences like reading books, watching documentaries, engaging in discussions, and practical hands-on experiences. Additionally, online platforms and digital resources have made learning more accessible than ever, offering courses, tutorials, and forums on virtually any topic imaginable. Embracing new learning opportunities means leveraging these diverse avenues to gain knowledge and skills.

Another key element of embracing new learning opportunities is the willingness to challenge and reassess one's existing beliefs and assumptions. This involves being open to new ideas and perspectives, even when they conflict with one's current understanding. It requires a degree of humility and the acknowledgment that one's knowledge is always incomplete and subject to change. This can be particularly important in professional settings, where staying current with industry trends and best practices is crucial. For example, a professional in the tech industry might need to continually learn about new programming languages, tools, and methodologies to stay competitive. Similarly, someone in the healthcare field might need to keep up with the latest research and treatments to provide the best care to their patients.

Embracing new learning opportunities also involves a willingness to take risks and embrace failure as part of the learning process. Trying new things often comes with the possibility of making mistakes or encountering setbacks. However, these experiences are valuable learning opportunities in themselves. They can provide insights into what works and what doesn't, helping individuals refine their skills and approaches. For example, an entrepreneur might try different business strategies and learn from the failures and successes of each. Similarly, a student might experiment with different study techniques to find the one that works best for them. Embracing failure as a learning opportunity helps build resilience and fosters a growth mindset, where challenges are seen as opportunities for development rather than insurmountable obstacles.

The process of embracing new learning opportunities is also closely tied to the development of critical thinking and problem-solving skills.

These skills are essential for analyzing information, making informed decisions, and tackling complex problems. Critical thinking involves questioning assumptions, evaluating evidence, and considering multiple perspectives. It is a key component of effective learning, as it allows individuals to not only absorb new information but also to understand and apply it in meaningful ways. For example, learning about a new scientific theory or historical event involves not just memorizing facts but also understanding the broader context, implications, and underlying principles. Similarly, problem-solving involves identifying challenges, generating potential solutions, and evaluating their effectiveness. These skills are applicable in virtually every area of life and are crucial for adapting to new situations and challenges.

In addition to individual benefits, embracing new learning opportunities can have a positive impact on personal relationships and community engagement. Learning new skills or gaining new knowledge can be a shared experience that brings people together, fostering stronger connections and mutual understanding. For example, learning a new language can open doors to new cultures and communities, enhancing cross-cultural communication and empathy. Similarly, participating in community-based learning initiatives, such as volunteer projects or local workshops, can strengthen social bonds and contribute to community development. By sharing what they learn with others, individuals can also inspire and encourage those around them to pursue their own learning journeys.

Moreover, embracing new learning opportunities can lead to increased creativity and innovation. Exposure to new ideas and perspectives can stimulate creative thinking and inspire new ways of approaching problems and challenges. This is particularly important in fields that require innovation, such as technology, arts, and entrepreneurship. For example, a designer who learns about new materials or techniques can expand their creative toolkit and develop unique designs. Similarly, an entrepreneur who explores new markets or business models can discover innovative ways to meet customer needs. In this way, continuous learning can be a key driver of creativity and innovation, both at an individual and organizational level.

The workplace is another area where embracing new learning opportunities is crucial. In today's fast-paced and ever-changing job market, staying relevant often requires continuous learning and upskilling. This can include learning new technical skills, developing leadership abilities, or staying up-to-date with industry trends and regulations. Many employers recognize the importance of continuous learning and offer professional development opportunities, such as training programs, workshops, and mentorship schemes. By taking advantage of these opportunities, employees can enhance their skills, increase their job satisfaction, and improve their career prospects. Additionally, organizations that foster a culture of learning and development are often more agile and adaptable, better equipped to respond to changes in the market and industry.

The concept of lifelong learning is central to the idea of embracing new learning opportunities. Lifelong learning is the ongoing, voluntary, and self-motivated pursuit of knowledge for personal or professional reasons. It emphasizes the importance of learning at all stages of life, not just during formal education. This approach to learning recognizes that the world is constantly changing and that continuous learning is essential for personal growth and adaptation. It encourages individuals to be proactive in seeking out new learning experiences and to view learning as an integral part of life. Whether through formal education, work experiences, hobbies, or personal exploration, lifelong learning provides a pathway to continual self-improvement and fulfillment.

Finally, embracing new learning opportunities can lead to a greater sense of purpose and fulfillment. Learning new things can be a deeply rewarding experience, providing a sense of accomplishment and satisfaction. It can also open up new possibilities and directions in life, whether through discovering a new passion, advancing in one's career, or contributing to personal and societal well-being. For example, learning about environmental sustainability might inspire someone to adopt more eco-friendly practices or get involved in conservation efforts. Similarly, learning about social issues might lead someone to become an advocate or volunteer for a cause they care about. In this way, embracing new learning opportunities can help individuals lead more meaningful and engaged lives.

Chapter 10: The Satisfaction of a Completed Checklist

The satisfaction of completing a checklist is a deeply ingrained aspect of human psychology, providing a sense of accomplishment and order. This feeling stems from several psychological factors and practical benefits that come with the act of checking off tasks. One of the primary reasons people derive satisfaction from completing checklists is the tangible evidence of progress. In a world where many accomplishments are abstract or long-term, checklists offer a concrete way to visualize and measure progress. Each checked item is a small victory, a visible sign that something has been achieved, no matter how minor it may seem. This visualization can be particularly motivating, serving as a reminder of what has been done and what remains to be accomplished.

Moreover, completing a checklist taps into the brain's reward system. Each time we check off an item, our brain releases dopamine, a neurotransmitter associated with pleasure and satisfaction. This release creates a positive feedback loop, reinforcing the behavior and making us more likely to engage in similar task-oriented activities in the future. This biological response can be likened to a small celebration, a momentary boost in mood and motivation that encourages continued effort and perseverance.

The act of creating and using a checklist also brings a sense of control and organization to our lives. In an often chaotic and unpredictable world, checklists provide structure and order. They help us prioritize tasks, allocate time and resources effectively, and manage our responsibilities systematically. This organization can reduce feelings of overwhelm and anxiety, as tasks are broken down into manageable parts. By clarifying what needs to be done and in what order, checklists can help prevent procrastination and improve productivity. The sense of control gained from this process can lead to increased confidence and a greater sense of agency in one's daily life.

Furthermore, checklists serve as a tool for self-reflection and personal growth. By regularly reviewing completed checklists, individuals can identify patterns in their productivity and time management. This reflection can highlight strengths and areas for improvement, providing valuable insights into personal habits and behaviors. Over time, this awareness can lead to more efficient work habits, better goal-setting, and a greater understanding of one's capabilities and limits. The ability to learn from past experiences, as captured in these checklists, is a key component of personal development.

In professional settings, the completion of checklists can also enhance team collaboration and communication. Shared checklists ensure that all team members are on the same page regarding project status, deadlines, and responsibilities. This transparency can prevent misunderstandings and ensure that everyone is working towards common goals. In addition, the sense of shared accomplishment when a team collectively completes a checklist can foster camaraderie and a positive work culture. Celebrating these small wins as a team can boost morale and strengthen interpersonal bonds, contributing to a more cohesive and motivated workforce.

Another important aspect of the satisfaction derived from completing checklists is the reinforcement of discipline and consistency. Regularly using checklists can help instill a disciplined approach to tasks, encouraging individuals to tackle even mundane or challenging activities. This discipline can spill over into other areas of life, fostering a general sense of diligence and commitment. Consistency in completing tasks also builds momentum, making it easier to maintain productivity over time. This momentum can be crucial for tackling larger projects or achieving long-term goals, as it breaks down the process into more manageable steps.

Moreover, checklists can serve as a form of self-care, offering a way to balance obligations and personal time. By clearly delineating work tasks and personal activities, individuals can ensure they are not neglecting self-care or leisure in favor of work. This balance is essential for overall well-being, as it helps prevent burnout and maintains a healthy work-life equilibrium. In this way, checklists can be a tool not only for productivity but also for maintaining a holistic approach to life, where work, rest, and recreation are all valued and attended to.

Finally, the act of checking off items on a list provides a moment of pause and reflection, a brief respite in a busy day. This pause allows individuals to acknowledge their efforts, appreciate their progress, and reset their focus for the tasks ahead. It is a moment of mindfulness that can bring clarity and calm, helping to center the mind and reduce stress. In an age where we are constantly bombarded with information and distractions, these moments of pause are increasingly valuable. They provide a space to breathe, to regroup, and to approach the next task with renewed energy and focus.

Chapter 11: Discovering Hidden Talents

Discovering hidden talents is a journey of self-discovery that often leads to personal growth, enhanced self-esteem, and a more fulfilling life. Hidden talents are abilities or skills that a person may possess but is not consciously aware of or has not fully developed. These talents can range from artistic abilities, such as painting or writing, to practical skills, like cooking or problem-solving, and even interpersonal talents, such as empathy or leadership. The process of uncovering these hidden abilities can be transformative, as it opens new avenues for self-expression, career opportunities, and personal satisfaction.

One of the first steps in discovering hidden talents is to cultivate a mindset of curiosity and openness. Many people limit their potential by adhering to a fixed set of beliefs about what they are capable of, often shaped by past experiences or societal expectations. By challenging these limiting beliefs and being open to trying new activities, individuals can explore unfamiliar territories where hidden talents may lie. This exploration requires a willingness to step out of one's comfort zone and embrace the possibility of failure as a learning experience rather than a setback. The journey of discovering hidden talents is often marked by trial and error, where each attempt provides valuable insights into one's abilities and interests.

Engaging in a variety of activities is another crucial aspect of uncovering hidden talents. Trying different hobbies, sports, artistic pursuits, or even volunteering for new roles at work or in the community can reveal latent skills. For example, someone who has never tried gardening might discover a natural affinity for it, leading to a newfound passion and skill set. Similarly, participating in a team sport could reveal leadership qualities or a knack for strategic thinking. These experiences not only help identify hidden talents but also contribute to a richer and more diverse skill set, enhancing overall personal development.

Feedback from others can also play a significant role in identifying hidden talents. Sometimes, talents are so innate or effortless that individuals may not recognize them as special. External feedback, whether from friends, family, colleagues, or mentors, can provide valuable perspectives. Others may notice skills or attributes that one takes for granted or sees as unremarkable. Encouragement and constructive feedback can boost confidence and motivate individuals to further develop these talents. Additionally, engaging in discussions with others about their talents and interests can provide inspiration and highlight areas worth exploring.

Another key element in discovering hidden talents is reflection and introspection. Taking the time to reflect on past experiences, achievements, and moments of joy can provide clues to hidden abilities. Journaling, meditating, or simply spending quiet time thinking about what activities make one feel energized and fulfilled can uncover passions and talents that might otherwise remain hidden. Reflecting on moments of success or satisfaction, even in small tasks, can reveal strengths that may not have been fully recognized. This process of introspection helps individuals understand their unique qualities and how they can be harnessed in various aspects of life.

Education and continuous learning are also vital in the process of discovering hidden talents. Engaging in lifelong learning, whether through formal education, online courses, workshops, or self-study, exposes individuals to new concepts and skills. This exposure can ignite interest in areas previously unexplored, revealing hidden talents in the process. For example, someone who takes a course in digital design may discover a flair for visual aesthetics and storytelling. Learning new skills not only broadens one's horizons but also provides the tools and knowledge necessary to nurture and develop newfound talents.

Sometimes, discovering hidden talents involves revisiting childhood interests or passions that were set aside as one grew older. As adults, people often prioritize practical concerns over personal interests, leading to the neglect of activities they once enjoyed. Reconnecting with these early passions can rekindle talents that have lain dormant. For instance, someone who loved drawing as a child but abandoned it due to other commitments might find that they still possess a talent for art. Rediscovering these old interests can bring joy and fulfillment, as well as a renewed sense of purpose and identity.

Moreover, hidden talents can sometimes emerge in response to challenges or adversity. Difficult situations often require individuals to tap into resources and abilities they may not have been aware of. For example, someone facing a personal crisis might discover a talent for resilience, problem-solving, or emotional intelligence. Similarly, taking on a challenging project at work or in a community setting can reveal leadership skills or creative thinking abilities. These experiences highlight the potential for growth and self-discovery in the face of obstacles and can lead to the recognition and development of new talents.

The process of developing hidden talents requires time, practice, and dedication. Once a talent is identified, it is important to cultivate it through regular practice and by seeking opportunities to apply it. Joining clubs, groups, or communities with similar interests can provide support, encouragement, and opportunities for growth. Mentorship and coaching can also be invaluable, offering guidance, feedback, and inspiration. By actively working on developing these talents, individuals can enhance their skills and gain confidence in their abilities.

The benefits of discovering hidden talents are manifold. On a personal level, it can lead to increased self-esteem and a greater sense of accomplishment and fulfillment. It can also open up new career opportunities, as talents often align with potential professional paths. For example, someone who discovers a talent for public speaking might pursue opportunities in teaching, leadership, or advocacy. Furthermore, discovering and developing hidden talents can enhance one's quality of life, providing new ways to engage with the world, connect with others, and express oneself creatively and authentically.

In summary, discovering hidden talents is a journey of exploration, reflection, and growth. It involves challenging limiting beliefs, trying new activities, seeking feedback, and reflecting on past experiences. Continuous learning, reconnecting with childhood interests, and facing challenges can also play a role in uncovering these talents. The process requires patience, practice, and a willingness to step out of one's comfort zone. The rewards, however, are significant, offering personal fulfillment, increased confidence, new career opportunities, and a richer, more engaged life. By embracing the journey of discovering hidden talents, individuals can unlock their full potential and live more authentically and meaningfully.

Chapter 12: Turning Setbacks into Opportunities

Turning setbacks into opportunities is a crucial skill that involves resilience, creativity, and a positive mindset. Setbacks are an inevitable part of life, affecting both personal and professional spheres. They can range from minor inconveniences to significant challenges, such as losing a job, facing a health issue, or encountering obstacles in achieving one's goals. While setbacks can be disheartening and challenging, they also offer valuable lessons and opportunities for growth. The ability to transform setbacks into opportunities involves a proactive approach to overcoming challenges, learning from experiences, and finding new pathways to success.

At the core of turning setbacks into opportunities is the concept of resilience. Resilience is the capacity to recover quickly from difficulties and adapt to changing circumstances. It involves maintaining a positive outlook and the ability to bounce back from adversity. Developing resilience begins with accepting that setbacks are a natural part of the journey. This acceptance allows individuals to process their emotions and view setbacks not as failures, but as temporary obstacles that can be overcome. Resilient individuals are better equipped to handle stress and are more likely to see setbacks as challenges to be faced rather than insurmountable barriers.

A crucial aspect of transforming setbacks into opportunities is reframing one's perspective. Reframing involves changing the way one perceives a situation, focusing on potential positive outcomes rather than negative aspects. For example, losing a job can be seen not just as a loss but as an opportunity to explore new career paths, acquire new skills, or even start a business. By shifting focus from the loss to the potential for growth, individuals can reduce the negative emotional impact of setbacks and open themselves up to new possibilities. This shift in mindset is essential for recognizing opportunities that may not be immediately apparent.

Setbacks often serve as catalysts for creativity and innovation. When faced with challenges, individuals are forced to think outside the box and find new solutions. This creative problem-solving can lead to the development of new skills, the discovery of untapped talents, or the identification of novel approaches to existing problems. For instance, an artist who loses access to traditional materials may experiment with new mediums, leading to unique and innovative works. Similarly, a business facing financial difficulties might find more efficient ways of operating or diversify its product offerings. The necessity to adapt can thus lead to significant advancements and improvements.

Another important element in turning setbacks into opportunities is learning from the experience. Setbacks provide a unique opportunity to reflect on what went wrong and why. This reflection can lead to valuable insights into one's actions, decisions, and circumstances. By analyzing setbacks, individuals can identify areas for improvement, develop new strategies, and avoid repeating the same mistakes in the future. This process of learning and self-improvement is fundamental to personal and professional growth. It enables individuals to emerge from setbacks stronger and more capable, with a deeper understanding of themselves and their goals.

In addition to personal growth, setbacks can also foster a sense of empathy and understanding toward others. Experiencing challenges can make individuals more compassionate and supportive, as they better understand the difficulties that others may face. This increased empathy can enhance relationships and build stronger communities. In professional settings, leaders who have experienced and overcome setbacks are often more effective in guiding and supporting their teams through difficult times. They can draw on their experiences to offer practical advice, encouragement, and motivation, fostering a positive and resilient work culture.

Turning setbacks into opportunities also involves taking proactive steps to address challenges. This means not only reacting to setbacks but actively seeking out opportunities for growth and improvement. For example, in response to a professional setback, an individual might pursue additional training, seek mentorship, or network with others in their field. These proactive measures can open up new career opportunities and expand one's professional horizons. Similarly, in response to a personal setback, such as a health issue, individuals might adopt healthier lifestyles, explore new hobbies, or focus on personal development. Taking control of the situation and making deliberate choices can lead to positive outcomes and a sense of empowerment.

Networking and building strong relationships can also play a vital role in transforming setbacks into opportunities. Supportive networks provide emotional support, practical advice, and resources that can help individuals navigate challenging times. Mentors, colleagues, friends, and family can offer different perspectives, helping to reframe setbacks and identify potential opportunities. Networking can also open doors to new opportunities, whether through job referrals, partnerships, or collaborations. Building and maintaining these relationships is crucial, as they can be a source of strength and inspiration during difficult periods.

Furthermore, setbacks can serve as a reminder of the importance of flexibility and adaptability. In a rapidly changing world, the ability to adapt to new circumstances is a key determinant of success. Flexibility involves being open to change, willing to revise plans, and capable of finding alternative paths to achieve one's goals. This adaptability not only helps individuals navigate setbacks but also prepares them for future challenges. It encourages a mindset of continuous learning and growth, where setbacks are seen as opportunities to evolve and improve.

Finally, it is important to celebrate the small victories that come from overcoming setbacks. Recognizing and appreciating progress, no matter how minor, can boost morale and reinforce a positive outlook. Celebrating achievements, such as mastering a new skill, securing a new job, or simply making it through a tough day, helps build confidence and motivation. These celebrations acknowledge the effort and resilience required to turn setbacks into opportunities and encourage continued perseverance.

Chapter 13: The Beauty of a Balanced Budget

The beauty of a balanced budget lies in its ability to bring stability, control, and peace of mind to both personal and organizational finances. A balanced budget, where income equals or exceeds expenses, serves as a fundamental pillar of financial health. It ensures that resources are allocated effectively, debts are managed responsibly, and future goals can be pursued without undue financial stress. The concept of a balanced budget extends beyond mere numbers; it embodies principles of discipline, foresight, and adaptability that are crucial for long-term success and well-being.

At its core, a balanced budget provides a clear and realistic picture of one's financial situation. It involves careful tracking of income and expenses, which helps in understanding spending habits and identifying areas where adjustments can be made. This awareness is the first step towards achieving financial control. For individuals, knowing exactly where money is coming from and where it is going can prevent the common pitfalls of overspending and debt accumulation. For businesses and organizations, a balanced budget is essential for sustainable operations, ensuring that expenditures are aligned with revenues and that resources are utilized efficiently.

One of the most significant benefits of maintaining a balanced budget is the reduction of financial stress. Financial instability is a major source of anxiety and can impact various aspects of life, including health, relationships, and overall well-being. By keeping expenses within the limits of available income, individuals and organizations can avoid the stress associated with debt and financial uncertainty. A balanced budget provides a sense of security, knowing that all obligations can be met without resorting to borrowing or other desperate measures. This financial stability enables individuals to focus on other important life aspects, such as personal development, career growth, and family.

Another key aspect of a balanced budget is its role in fostering financial discipline. Creating and sticking to a budget requires setting priorities, making conscious spending choices, and sometimes making sacrifices. This discipline is a crucial skill that extends beyond finances, promoting responsible behavior and decision-making in other areas of life. For instance, the practice of budgeting can teach valuable lessons about delayed gratification, where immediate desires are postponed in favor of long-term benefits. This principle is applicable not only to financial decisions but also to other pursuits, such as education, career planning, and personal development.

A balanced budget also lays the foundation for saving and investing, which are critical components of long-term financial planning. By ensuring that income exceeds expenses, a balanced budget creates surplus funds that can be allocated towards savings and investments. This surplus acts as a financial cushion, providing protection against unexpected expenses or emergencies. Over time, consistent saving and investing can lead to significant wealth accumulation, enabling individuals to achieve major financial goals such as buying a home, funding education, or securing retirement. For organizations, surplus funds can be reinvested into the business, fueling growth and innovation.

In addition to providing financial security, a balanced budget enables greater flexibility and adaptability. Life is unpredictable, and unexpected expenses or changes in income can occur at any time. A well-balanced budget includes provisions for such contingencies, often in the form of an emergency fund. This fund acts as a buffer, allowing individuals and organizations to navigate unforeseen financial challenges without derailing their overall financial plan. This adaptability is particularly important in times of economic uncertainty, such as during recessions or market downturns, where having a financial safety net can make a significant difference.

Moreover, a balanced budget encourages goal-setting and strategic planning. By clearly defining financial resources and obligations, it becomes easier to set realistic and achievable financial goals. These goals can range from short-term objectives, such as saving for a vacation, to long-term aspirations, such as purchasing a home or retiring comfortably. The process of budgeting forces individuals and organizations to prioritize these goals, allocate resources accordingly, and track progress over time. This structured approach not only helps in achieving financial objectives but also instills a sense of purpose and direction.

In the context of businesses and public organizations, a balanced budget is crucial for maintaining credibility and trust with stakeholders. For businesses, a balanced budget signals financial health and stability to investors, creditors, and employees, fostering confidence and attracting investment. It demonstrates that the business is being managed responsibly and is capable of meeting its financial obligations. For public organizations, such as governments or non-profits, a balanced budget is essential for maintaining public trust and accountability. It ensures that taxpayer money or donations are being used efficiently and that the organization is operating within its means.

A balanced budget also contributes to economic stability at a broader level. When individuals, businesses, and governments manage their finances responsibly, it reduces the likelihood of financial crises, such as bankruptcies or defaults. This stability is beneficial for the overall economy, as it promotes steady growth, reduces volatility, and fosters a healthy financial environment. For governments, maintaining a balanced budget or minimizing deficits is crucial for managing public debt levels, controlling inflation, and ensuring that resources are available for essential services and infrastructure.

Furthermore, the process of budgeting can lead to greater financial literacy. Creating and maintaining a budget requires an understanding of financial concepts such as income, expenses, savings, debt, and investments. This knowledge empowers individuals to make informed financial decisions, avoid common pitfalls such as excessive debt, and take proactive steps toward financial security. Financial literacy is an invaluable skill in today's complex economic landscape, where individuals are increasingly responsible for their financial well-being.

Chapter 14: Nurturing Relationships

Nurturing relationships is an essential aspect of human life, deeply rooted in our nature as social beings. Whether personal, professional, or communal, relationships form the bedrock of our existence, providing support, companionship, and a sense of belonging. Nurturing these relationships involves a conscious effort to cultivate and maintain connections, characterized by trust, communication, empathy, and mutual respect. The process of nurturing relationships is ongoing and requires attention, patience, and intentional actions that contribute to the health and longevity of these bonds. Understanding the importance and methods of nurturing relationships can significantly enhance the quality of our lives, fostering a sense of fulfillment, happiness, and emotional well-being.

One of the foundational elements of nurturing relationships is effective communication. Communication is the means by which individuals share thoughts, feelings, and experiences, creating a bridge of understanding and connection. Open and honest communication allows individuals to express their needs, desires, and concerns, reducing misunderstandings and conflicts. It involves not just speaking, but also listening actively and empathetically. Active listening means fully concentrating, understanding, and responding to the speaker, showing that their perspective is valued. This form of communication fosters trust and intimacy, essential for deep and meaningful relationships. In both personal and professional contexts, effective communication can prevent conflicts, resolve issues, and build stronger connections.

Empathy, the ability to understand and share the feelings of another, is another crucial component of nurturing relationships. Empathy allows individuals to connect on a deeper emotional level, offering support and comfort during times of need. It involves recognizing and validating the emotions of others, showing compassion and understanding without judgment. Empathy strengthens relationships by fostering a sense of solidarity and mutual care. It encourages a supportive environment where individuals feel safe to express themselves and share their experiences. In professional settings, empathetic leadership and teamwork can enhance collaboration, boost morale, and create a positive workplace culture.

Trust is another vital element in nurturing relationships. Trust is built over time through consistent actions that demonstrate reliability, honesty, and integrity. It is the foundation upon which all healthy relationships are built, enabling individuals to feel secure and confident in their interactions with others. Trust fosters a sense of safety and openness, allowing individuals to be vulnerable and authentic without fear of betrayal or judgment. Maintaining trust requires a commitment to honesty, keeping promises, and being accountable for one's actions. When trust is established, it creates a strong bond that can withstand challenges and conflicts, making relationships more resilient and enduring.

Mutual respect is essential for nurturing relationships, as it acknowledges the inherent worth and dignity of each individual. Respect involves recognizing and valuing the differences in others, including their opinions, beliefs, and boundaries. It is about treating others with consideration and courtesy, even in disagreements. Mutual respect fosters a positive and inclusive environment where individuals feel appreciated and valued for who they are. In relationships, respect can manifest in various ways, such as honoring commitments, giving credit where it's due, and being mindful of each other's time and space. Respectful interactions build a foundation of equality and fairness, crucial for sustaining healthy and harmonious relationships.

Another important aspect of nurturing relationships is the act of giving and receiving support. Support can take many forms, including emotional, practical, or even financial assistance. Being supportive means being present for others during difficult times, offering encouragement, and providing help when needed. It also involves recognizing when to seek support, understanding that relationships are reciprocal and that everyone benefits from mutual care and assistance. The exchange of support strengthens the bond between individuals, fostering a sense of community and interdependence. It creates a network of care that enhances resilience and helps individuals navigate life's challenges more effectively.

Quality time is a key ingredient in nurturing relationships. Spending time together, whether through shared activities, conversations, or simply being present, helps strengthen the connection between individuals. Quality time fosters intimacy and allows for the deepening of understanding and appreciation for one another. It is an opportunity to create shared experiences and memories, which can reinforce the bond and provide a foundation for a lasting relationship. In today's fast-paced world, where time is often scarce, prioritizing quality time with loved ones can be a powerful way to nurture and sustain relationships. This can involve simple acts like sharing meals, enjoying hobbies together, or engaging in meaningful conversations.

Forgiveness is a crucial element in maintaining and nurturing relationships. Conflicts and misunderstandings are inevitable in any relationship, but the ability to forgive can help repair and strengthen bonds. Forgiveness involves letting go of grudges, resentment, and the desire for retribution, allowing individuals to move past conflicts and focus on the positive aspects of the relationship. It requires empathy, understanding, and a willingness to see things from the other person's perspective. Forgiveness is not about condoning harmful behavior but rather about releasing the emotional burden associated with it. It is a powerful tool for healing and can lead to renewed trust and a deeper connection.

Commitment is also fundamental to nurturing relationships. A commitment to a relationship means being dedicated to its growth and well-being, even during challenging times. It involves making conscious choices to invest time, energy, and resources into the relationship, prioritizing it over other competing interests. Commitment provides stability and assurance, creating a sense of security and belonging. It is the foundation upon which individuals can build a future together, whether in personal relationships, such as marriage or friendship, or professional relationships, such as partnerships or team collaborations. Demonstrating commitment can take many forms, including consistent communication, supporting each other's goals, and being present in both good times and bad.

Personal growth and self-awareness play a significant role in nurturing relationships. Understanding oneself, including one's strengths, weaknesses, and emotional triggers, can improve how we relate to others. Self-awareness helps individuals communicate more effectively, set healthy boundaries, and manage conflicts constructively. Personal growth involves ongoing learning and development, both individually and within the context of relationships. It encourages individuals to be open to feedback, willing to change, and committed to becoming better partners, friends, or colleagues. By fostering self-awareness and personal growth, individuals can contribute more positively to their relationships, enhancing their quality and longevity.

In addition to individual efforts, nurturing relationships often requires collective and community support. Family, friends, and social networks can play a crucial role in supporting and sustaining relationships. They provide a broader context of care and connection, offering resources, advice, and encouragement. Engaging with a supportive community can strengthen individual relationships by providing a sense of belonging and shared purpose. It also offers opportunities to learn from others' experiences, gain new perspectives, and develop social skills. Community engagement can enrich relationships, providing a broader social fabric that supports personal and collective well-being.

Chapter 15: Enjoying a Homemade Meal

Enjoying a homemade meal is a delightful experience that offers a multitude of sensory and emotional pleasures, encompassing more than just the act of eating. It is a celebration of flavors, aromas, textures, and the joy of creating something nourishing and delicious from scratch. Homemade meals often carry a sense of tradition, culture, and personal touch, making them unique and special. The process of preparing and enjoying a homemade meal can be a fulfilling and therapeutic experience, fostering a sense of accomplishment, connection, and well-being. This experience is enriched by the knowledge of the effort, care, and creativity that goes into cooking, making every bite not just about sustenance but also about pleasure and meaning.

One of the primary joys of enjoying a homemade meal is the sheer variety and customization it offers. Cooking at home allows for complete control over the ingredients, flavors, and presentation of the food. This control means that meals can be tailored to suit personal tastes, dietary preferences, and nutritional needs. Whether someone prefers spicy, sweet, savory, or a combination of flavors, homemade meals can be adjusted accordingly. This level of customization is particularly valuable for individuals with specific dietary requirements, such as allergies, intolerances, or health conditions that necessitate certain food choices. The ability to create a meal that is perfectly suited to one's preferences and needs enhances the enjoyment and satisfaction derived from eating.

The process of cooking a homemade meal itself is a rich and rewarding experience. It involves a series of creative and technical steps, from planning and shopping for ingredients to preparing, cooking, and presenting the food. Each step provides an opportunity for learning, experimentation, and expression. For many, cooking is a form of art, where ingredients are the palette and the kitchen is the studio. The transformation of raw ingredients into a cohesive and delicious dish is a process that engages the senses and stimulates the mind. The aromas of spices, the sizzle of ingredients on the stove, and the vibrant colors of fresh produce all contribute to the sensory pleasure of cooking. This sensory engagement can be deeply satisfying, providing a form of mindfulness and relaxation.

Homemade meals are often imbued with cultural and familial significance, carrying traditions and memories that enhance their value. Recipes passed down through generations or dishes associated with special occasions can evoke feelings of nostalgia and connection. These meals often tell stories, reflecting the history and identity of a family or community. Sharing a homemade meal can thus be a way of honoring heritage, preserving cultural practices, and fostering a sense of belonging. This cultural aspect of homemade meals adds an additional layer of enjoyment, as it connects individuals to their roots and strengthens bonds with loved ones. Cooking and sharing traditional dishes can be a way of keeping cultural traditions alive, especially in an increasingly globalized world where such practices may otherwise fade.

The nutritional benefits of homemade meals are another significant aspect of their appeal. Cooking at home allows for greater control over the nutritional content of meals, including the quality and quantity of ingredients. This control can lead to healthier eating habits, as home-cooked meals often contain fewer processed ingredients, added sugars, and unhealthy fats compared to restaurant or pre-packaged foods. The use of fresh, whole ingredients ensures that meals are rich in essential nutrients, such as vitamins, minerals, and fiber. Additionally, portion control is easier to manage at home, helping to avoid overeating. The combination of healthier ingredients and appropriate portions contributes to overall well-being and can help prevent diet-related health issues such as obesity, diabetes, and heart disease.

The economic aspect of homemade meals also contributes to their appeal. Cooking at home is generally more cost-effective than dining out or buying pre-packaged meals. By purchasing raw ingredients and preparing them at home, individuals can save money while also reducing food waste. This financial benefit is particularly significant for families or individuals on a budget, as it allows for the preparation of nutritious and satisfying meals without overspending. The cost-effectiveness of homemade meals extends beyond the immediate savings, as healthier eating habits can lead to reduced medical expenses and improved long-term health outcomes.

Homemade meals also offer a wonderful opportunity for social interaction and bonding. The act of cooking and sharing food brings people together, creating a sense of community and togetherness. Whether it's cooking with family members, hosting a dinner party with friends, or simply sharing a meal with a partner, these moments foster connection and intimacy. Cooking and eating together can strengthen relationships, provide a space for meaningful conversations, and create lasting memories. For families, involving children in the cooking process can be a way to teach them valuable life skills, instill healthy eating habits, and create cherished family traditions.

The environmental impact of homemade meals is another important consideration. Cooking at home can be more environmentally friendly than dining out or relying on processed foods, which often involve significant packaging and transportation. By choosing locally sourced, seasonal ingredients and reducing reliance on processed foods, individuals can lower their carbon footprint. Additionally, home cooking allows for better management of food waste, as portions can be controlled and leftovers can be repurposed in creative ways. This mindful approach to food consumption aligns with sustainable living practices, promoting a more responsible and conscious relationship with food and the environment.

Chapter 16: The Magic of Decluttering

The magic of decluttering lies in its transformative power to bring order, clarity, and peace into our lives. At its core, decluttering is the process of removing unnecessary items from our living and working spaces, which can lead to a profound sense of liberation and renewal. While it may seem like a simple task of tidying up, decluttering often has far-reaching effects on our mental and emotional well-being, relationships, productivity, and overall quality of life. The act of decluttering goes beyond physical organization; it involves a thoughtful evaluation of what we value and prioritize, encouraging us to let go of what no longer serves us. This process can lead to a more intentional and fulfilling life, where we are surrounded only by things that bring us joy, utility, or meaning.

One of the most immediate benefits of decluttering is the creation of a more organized and aesthetically pleasing environment. A cluttered space can be visually overwhelming and distracting, making it difficult to focus and relax. By removing excess items and organizing what remains, we create a cleaner, more harmonious environment that promotes a sense of calm and well-being. This physical transformation can have a significant impact on our mood and mindset, as our surroundings often reflect and influence our internal state. A tidy, well-organized space can foster a sense of order and control, reducing feelings of stress and anxiety.

The process of decluttering also encourages mindfulness and intentionality. As we go through our belongings, we are prompted to reflect on what we truly need and value. This reflection helps us distinguish between essential and non-essential items, making us more conscious of our consumption habits. Decluttering challenges us to confront the reasons we accumulate things—whether out of habit, emotional attachment, or societal pressure—and encourages us to adopt a more mindful approach to acquiring new possessions. This mindfulness extends beyond physical objects, influencing how we spend our time, energy, and resources. By prioritizing what truly matters, we can focus more on experiences and relationships that enrich our lives, rather than being bogged down by material excess.

Another profound aspect of decluttering is the emotional and psychological release it can provide. Many people accumulate items due to emotional attachments or out of a fear of letting go. However, holding on to unnecessary belongings can lead to feelings of overwhelm and guilt, especially when these items are associated with past memories, unfulfilled aspirations, or missed opportunities. Decluttering offers a way to confront and process these emotions, allowing us to let go of the past and make space for new possibilities. This act of letting go can be incredibly freeing, helping us to release emotional baggage and move forward with a lighter, more positive mindset.

Decluttering can also enhance our productivity and efficiency. In a cluttered environment, finding necessary items can be time-consuming and frustrating, leading to wasted time and decreased productivity. An organized space, on the other hand, facilitates easier access to what we need, enabling us to work more efficiently and effectively. This is particularly important in workspaces, where an organized environment can contribute to better focus, creativity, and overall performance. By reducing the clutter around us, we minimize distractions and create a more conducive setting for concentration and productivity.

The benefits of decluttering extend to our relationships as well. Clutter can create tension and conflict within households, especially when different members have different levels of tolerance for disorganization. Decluttering as a family or household can be a collaborative effort that fosters communication, cooperation, and mutual respect. It can also be an opportunity to involve children in organizing and decision-making processes, teaching them valuable life skills such as responsibility, organization, and the importance of maintaining a tidy living space. In a broader social context, decluttering can lead to a sense of community and generosity. Donating unwanted items to charity or sharing them with friends and neighbors can foster connections and a sense of goodwill.

Financial benefits are another significant aspect of the magic of decluttering. By becoming more mindful of our possessions and consumption habits, we can reduce unnecessary spending and avoid the accumulation of debt. Decluttering helps us recognize the difference between wants and needs, encouraging more thoughtful and intentional purchasing decisions. This awareness can lead to significant savings and a more sustainable lifestyle. Moreover, selling unwanted items can provide additional income, which can be redirected towards savings, investments, or experiences that bring greater joy and fulfillment.

Decluttering can also have a positive impact on the environment. By reducing our consumption and making more intentional purchasing choices, we contribute to less waste and a lower carbon footprint. Donating or recycling items rather than discarding them reduces landfill waste and supports a circular economy. Decluttering encourages us to adopt a more sustainable mindset, where we prioritize quality over quantity and consider the long-term impact of our choices on the planet. This environmental consciousness aligns with broader movements towards minimalism and sustainability, promoting a lifestyle that is not only beneficial for individuals but also for the world at large.

The magic of decluttering is also evident in the way it can transform our approach to life's transitions and changes. Life events such as moving, downsizing, or significant life changes often necessitate decluttering. While these transitions can be challenging, they also present an opportunity to reassess and realign our possessions with our current needs and values. Decluttering during these times can ease the transition, making it more manageable and less stressful. It allows us to let go of the past and embrace the present, focusing on what is truly important in our lives. This adaptability and willingness to change are key components of personal growth and resilience.

Chapter 17: The Reward of a Good Workout

The reward of a good workout extends far beyond the immediate physical exertion and encompasses a wide range of benefits that enhance overall well-being. A good workout can leave one feeling invigorated, accomplished, and refreshed, serving as a powerful antidote to the stresses and challenges of daily life. The rewards of regular physical activity are multifaceted, impacting physical health, mental well-being, emotional stability, and social connections. Engaging in a good workout, whether it be through cardiovascular exercise, strength training, flexibility exercises, or a combination of these, offers a comprehensive approach to maintaining and improving health. The physical benefits include enhanced cardiovascular health, improved muscle strength and endurance, weight management, and increased flexibility. These improvements contribute to a higher quality of life by enabling individuals to perform daily activities with greater ease and reducing the risk of chronic diseases.

A good workout also has profound effects on mental health. Physical activity triggers the release of endorphins, often referred to as "feel-good" hormones, which can lead to an improved mood and a sense of euphoria, commonly known as a "runner's high." This chemical response in the brain helps alleviate symptoms of depression, anxiety, and stress, providing a natural and effective way to enhance mental well-being. Regular exercise has been shown to improve cognitive function, boost memory, and enhance concentration and mental clarity. These cognitive benefits are particularly valuable in today's fast-paced world, where mental sharpness and the ability to manage multiple tasks are essential. Furthermore, the routine and structure provided by a consistent workout regimen can instill a sense of discipline and accomplishment, contributing to improved self-esteem and confidence.

The emotional rewards of a good workout are equally significant. Exercise can serve as a powerful outlet for releasing pent-up emotions and stress, offering a constructive way to cope with life's challenges. The sense of achievement that comes from completing a workout, especially one that is challenging or pushes one's limits, can foster a sense of pride and resilience. This feeling of accomplishment can translate into other areas of life, encouraging a proactive and positive attitude toward tackling obstacles and pursuing goals. Moreover, exercise can be a time for introspection and mindfulness, allowing individuals to connect with themselves and process their thoughts and emotions in a healthy and productive manner.

Social connections are another rewarding aspect of a good workout. Many people find that participating in group exercise classes, sports teams, or fitness clubs provides a sense of community and camaraderie. These social interactions can be motivating and supportive, helping individuals stay committed to their fitness goals. The shared experience of working towards similar goals can strengthen bonds and foster new friendships, providing both emotional and social benefits. Additionally, for those who may feel isolated or lonely, joining a fitness community can offer a valuable sense of belonging and connection. These social aspects of exercise contribute to a more enjoyable and sustainable fitness routine, making it easier to maintain long-term commitments to health and wellness.

The rewards of a good workout are not limited to immediate physical and psychological benefits; they also contribute to long-term health and longevity. Regular physical activity is a key factor in preventing and managing a wide range of chronic diseases, including heart disease, diabetes, obesity, and certain types of cancer. By improving cardiovascular health, regulating blood sugar levels, and maintaining a healthy weight, exercise plays a crucial role in reducing the risk of these conditions. Additionally, regular workouts can enhance immune function, making the body more resilient to infections and illnesses. The cumulative effect of these health benefits is a longer, healthier life with a reduced burden of disease and disability.

The aesthetic benefits of a good workout, such as improved muscle tone, weight loss, and a more defined physique, are often a motivating factor for many individuals. These changes can enhance body image and self-confidence, contributing to a more positive self-perception. While aesthetic goals can be a valid and motivating aspect of exercise, it is important to recognize that the deeper, more intrinsic rewards of physical activity are what sustain long-term commitment and satisfaction. Focusing solely on external outcomes can sometimes lead to disappointment or unhealthy behaviors, whereas valuing the comprehensive benefits of exercise fosters a more balanced and fulfilling approach to fitness.

The adaptability and versatility of exercise are additional rewards of a good workout. There is a vast array of physical activities to choose from, allowing individuals to find what best suits their preferences, abilities, and goals. Whether it is running, swimming, yoga, weightlifting, dancing, or hiking, the diversity of exercise options ensures that there is something for everyone. This variety not only prevents boredom but also allows for a holistic approach to fitness, targeting different aspects of physical health, such as endurance, strength, flexibility, and balance. The ability to adapt workouts to different settings, such as indoors or outdoors, and different levels of intensity ensures that exercise can be integrated into a wide range of lifestyles and schedules.

Another important aspect of the reward of a good workout is the development of resilience and perseverance. Consistently engaging in physical activity, especially when it involves pushing through challenges or discomfort, can build mental toughness and a strong work ethic. The discipline required to stick to a workout regimen can spill over into other areas of life, fostering a greater sense of accountability and determination. This resilience is valuable not only in achieving fitness goals but also in navigating life's broader challenges, whether personal, professional, or academic. The process of setting goals, working towards them, and celebrating progress cultivates a growth mindset, encouraging continuous self-improvement and learning.

In summary, the reward of a good workout is a multifaceted experience that enhances physical, mental, emotional, and social well-being. The physical benefits, such as improved health, strength, and endurance, are complemented by significant mental health improvements, including reduced stress and enhanced cognitive function. Emotional rewards, such as increased self-esteem and emotional resilience, are augmented by the social connections and community that often accompany regular exercise. The long-term health benefits contribute to a higher quality of life and longevity, while the aesthetic improvements can boost body image and confidence. The adaptability, versatility, and resilience developed through regular workouts further underscore the comprehensive rewards of physical activity. Embracing the holistic benefits of exercise can lead to a more balanced, fulfilling, and healthy life, making the effort and commitment to a regular workout routine truly rewarding in every sense.

Chapter 18: Finding Peace in Meditation

Finding peace in meditation is a profound experience that offers a sanctuary from the chaos and demands of daily life. Meditation, a practice that involves focusing the mind and eliminating distractions, is widely recognized for its ability to cultivate inner calm, clarity, and emotional resilience. This ancient practice, which has roots in various spiritual and philosophical traditions, has gained widespread popularity in the modern world as a powerful tool for enhancing mental and emotional well-being. The peace found in meditation is not merely a temporary respite; it can transform one's outlook on life, foster deeper self-awareness, and promote a lasting sense of tranquility and balance.

The practice of meditation begins with creating a quiet, comfortable space, either physically or mentally, where one can sit or lie down without interruption. The posture may vary, but it often involves sitting comfortably with an upright spine, relaxed shoulders, and hands resting on the lap or knees. The eyes can be closed or softly focused, and the attention is gently directed inward. A fundamental aspect of meditation is the focus on the breath, which serves as an anchor to the present moment. By observing the breath's natural rhythm—its rise and fall, the sensation of air entering and leaving the nostrils—one cultivates mindfulness, a state of heightened awareness and presence.

As the mind settles, thoughts inevitably arise, often pulling attention away from the breath. This wandering of the mind is a natural part of the meditation process and presents an opportunity for cultivating awareness and compassion. Instead of becoming frustrated or judgmental, meditators are encouraged to acknowledge these thoughts without attachment or aversion, gently guiding their focus back to the breath. This practice of non-judgmental awareness helps to develop equanimity, the ability to remain calm and balanced in the face of internal and external disturbances. Over time, this equanimity extends beyond the meditation session, influencing how one responds to life's challenges and stresses.

The peace experienced during meditation is often described as a deep, abiding stillness, a state where the mind is free from the usual chatter and noise. This stillness allows for a greater sense of connection with one's true self, beyond the roles, identities, and narratives that typically define daily existence. In this space of inner quiet, individuals can explore the depths of their consciousness, gaining insights into their thoughts, emotions, and behaviors. This self-reflection fosters a greater understanding of one's motivations and patterns, leading to more intentional and mindful living.

The physiological benefits of meditation contribute significantly to the sense of peace it provides. Regular meditation practice has been shown to reduce stress by lowering cortisol levels, the hormone associated with stress response. It also activates the parasympathetic nervous system, which promotes relaxation and recovery. This physiological shift can lead to a reduction in symptoms of anxiety, depression, and other stress-related conditions. The relaxation response triggered by meditation also improves heart rate variability, blood pressure, and overall cardiovascular health, further enhancing the body's capacity to manage stress.

Emotional regulation is another key benefit of meditation, which directly contributes to finding peace. Through the practice of observing thoughts and feelings without attachment, meditators learn to detach from the reactive patterns that often govern their responses to emotional stimuli. This detachment does not imply indifference but rather a conscious choice to respond with clarity and compassion instead of being swept away by strong emotions. This heightened emotional awareness and control can lead to more harmonious relationships, improved communication, and a greater ability to cope with life's ups and downs. The cultivation of compassion, both for oneself and others, is a natural extension of this emotional regulation, promoting a more empathetic and understanding perspective.

Meditation also nurtures a sense of connection and oneness with the world. As individuals practice mindfulness, they become more attuned to the present moment and the interconnectedness of all life. This awareness can lead to a deeper appreciation for nature, relationships, and the simple joys of life. The sense of unity and interconnectedness fostered by meditation helps dissolve the illusion of separation and isolation, which is often a source of suffering. This realization can inspire a more altruistic and service-oriented approach to life, where the well-being of others becomes integral to one's own peace and happiness.

In addition to personal benefits, the peace found in meditation can have a ripple effect on society. Individuals who meditate regularly often exhibit qualities such as patience, empathy, and kindness, which positively influence their interactions with others. This shift in behavior can contribute to more peaceful and compassionate communities, where conflicts are resolved with greater understanding and cooperation. Moreover, the increased mindfulness and presence cultivated through meditation can lead to more thoughtful and responsible actions, promoting sustainability and ethical considerations in daily choices.

The transformative power of meditation is not limited to the periods of formal practice. The skills developed during meditation, such as mindfulness, awareness, and emotional regulation, can be applied throughout daily life. This integration of mindfulness into everyday activities—such as eating, walking, working, and interacting with others—further extends the sense of peace and presence cultivated in meditation. It encourages living in the moment and appreciating the beauty and richness of life as it unfolds, rather than being preoccupied with the past or anxious about the future.

The journey of finding peace in meditation is deeply personal and varies for each individual. Some may find immediate calm and clarity, while others may experience initial discomfort or restlessness as they confront suppressed emotions or ingrained thought patterns. However, with patience and persistence, the practice of meditation can lead to profound shifts in consciousness and a lasting sense of peace. It is important to approach meditation with an open and non-judgmental attitude, allowing the process to unfold naturally and accepting whatever arises during practice.

Chapter 19: The Delight of Finishing a Book

The delight of finishing a book is a multifaceted experience that touches upon a range of emotions, intellectual satisfaction, and personal achievement. When you turn the last page of a book, especially one that has captivated your interest and imagination, there is a profound sense of completion that settles over you. This feeling is akin to the satisfaction of completing a long journey, where each chapter represents a leg of the trip, and finishing the book is akin to arriving at your destination.

At the heart of this delight is the intellectual and emotional investment made during the reading process. From the moment you pick up a book, you embark on a journey of discovery. Characters become companions, their stories intertwined with your thoughts and emotions. The settings painted by the author transport you to different worlds, whether they are realms of fantasy, distant historical periods, or familiar contemporary landscapes. As you progress, you become more deeply involved, and the characters' triumphs and tribulations evoke responses that are intensely personal. The act of finishing the book provides closure to these relationships and narratives, allowing you to savor the entire arc of the story and reflect on its broader meanings.

The satisfaction of finishing a book is also rooted in the achievement of completing a task. In an age where distractions are plentiful and time often feels fragmented, dedicating yourself to the sustained effort required to finish a book is an accomplishment in itself. It signifies a commitment to intellectual growth and a devotion to nurturing one's mind. Each book read represents a milestone in a lifelong journey of learning and self-improvement. This sense of achievement is particularly pronounced when the book is challenging, either in its content or its length. Overcoming complex themes, dense prose, or extensive volumes adds an extra layer of accomplishment to the experience, underscoring your capacity for perseverance and critical engagement.

Finishing a book also opens up new avenues for reflection and discussion. The themes and ideas explored within its pages linger in your mind, prompting contemplation and sometimes even a reevaluation of your perspectives. Books often introduce you to new concepts, cultures, and philosophies, broadening your understanding of the world and your place within it. This intellectual expansion is a source of joy and pride, as it represents growth and the acquisition of knowledge. Furthermore, completing a book allows you to share your thoughts and insights with others, whether through casual conversations, book clubs, or online forums. These discussions can enhance your appreciation of the book and provide new insights that deepen your understanding.

The act of finishing a book also triggers a nostalgic reflection on the journey you have undertaken. As you close the final chapter, you might find yourself recalling the initial excitement of starting the book, the twists and turns of the plot, and the emotional highs and lows experienced along the way. This retrospection is a form of savoring the experience, akin to looking back on a memorable trip or an important life event. The book becomes a part of your personal history, a marker of a particular time and place in your life. This sense of nostalgia is often accompanied by a bittersweet feeling of parting from the characters and the world you have come to know so well, underscoring the depth of the connection forged through reading.

Moreover, the delight of finishing a book is amplified by the anticipation of what comes next. The conclusion of one book signals the beginning of another, each with the potential to offer new adventures, insights, and pleasures. This cyclical nature of reading ensures that the end of one journey is always the prelude to another, keeping the joy of discovery and learning perpetually alive. The moment of closing one book is often followed by the excitement of selecting the next, whether from a teetering stack on your bedside table, a well-curated bookstore, or an extensive digital library. This anticipation is a testament to the enduring allure of books and the infinite possibilities they hold.

Finishing a book also contributes to your personal narrative and sense of identity. Each book you read becomes a part of you, shaping your thoughts, beliefs, and values. The completion of a book can be a transformative experience, offering new insights or solidifying your understanding of certain concepts. This transformation is part of the ongoing process of self-discovery and personal growth. As you accumulate these experiences, you build a richer, more nuanced worldview, each book adding layers to your intellectual and emotional fabric. This continuous evolution is a source of deep satisfaction and pride, as it reflects your journey through life as a thoughtful, curious, and engaged individual.

In essence, the delight of finishing a book is a rich and rewarding experience that encompasses emotional fulfillment, intellectual satisfaction, personal achievement, and the joy of continuous discovery. It is a moment that celebrates the power of storytelling and the enduring human desire to explore, learn, and grow. Each book completed is a testament to your curiosity, dedication, and love for the written word, marking a significant milestone in your lifelong journey of reading and learning.

Chapter 20: The Accomplishment of a DIY Project

The accomplishment of a DIY (Do It Yourself) project is a deeply gratifying experience that resonates on multiple levels, from the tangible creation of something unique to the intangible rewards of self-sufficiency, creativity, and personal growth. When you complete a DIY project, you immerse yourself in a process that is both challenging and rewarding, engaging not just your hands but also your mind and heart. This experience starts with an idea or inspiration, often sparked by a need or a desire to create something functional, beautiful, or both. The journey from concept to completion is a transformative one, filled with learning, problem-solving, and the eventual satisfaction of seeing your vision come to life.

At the core of the DIY experience is the empowerment that comes from creating something with your own hands. In a world where mass-produced items are readily available, the ability to craft something unique stands out as a significant achievement. This empowerment begins with the initial planning stages, where you conceptualize your project, gather materials, and perhaps consult resources or tutorials. The sense of autonomy in choosing materials, colors, and designs according to your personal preferences is liberating. It allows for the expression of individuality and creativity, transforming a simple idea into a personalized artifact.

As you move into the execution phase, the hands-on work becomes a meditative process. Each step, whether it's measuring, cutting, assembling, or painting, demands attention to detail and precision. This focus can be deeply absorbing, providing a respite from the constant barrage of distractions in modern life. The physical act of working with tools and materials connects you to a long tradition of craftsmanship, invoking a sense of continuity with those who have built and created before you. This tactile engagement also reinforces the value of patience and perseverance, as DIY projects often involve trial and error, adjustments, and moments of frustration. Overcoming these challenges strengthens problem-solving skills and fosters a growth mindset, teaching that persistence and resilience are key to achieving goals.

The educational aspect of DIY projects cannot be overstated. Each project is an opportunity to learn new skills or improve existing ones. Whether you're delving into woodworking, electronics, sewing, or gardening, you acquire knowledge that is both practical and satisfying. This learning extends beyond technical skills; it includes understanding materials, tools, and techniques that can be applied to future projects. The process of learning by doing is incredibly effective, as it embeds knowledge through direct experience. This hands-on education not only builds competence but also confidence, as you prove to yourself that you are capable of tackling new and unfamiliar tasks.

One of the most rewarding aspects of completing a DIY project is the visible, tangible result of your efforts. The finished product stands as a testament to your hard work, creativity, and dedication. This sense of accomplishment is profoundly satisfying, as it provides clear evidence of your capabilities and the value of your efforts. Unlike many other forms of work where results can be abstract or delayed, the outcome of a DIY project is immediate and concrete. Whether it's a piece of furniture, a renovated room, a handcrafted gift, or a garden feature, the end result is something you can see, touch, and use. This tangible success reinforces the intrinsic rewards of creativity and self-reliance, fostering a sense of pride and fulfillment.

The accomplishment of a DIY project also brings significant emotional rewards. The process of creating something from scratch is inherently joyful, as it taps into the fundamental human drive to build and create. This joy is amplified when the project involves elements of personal significance, such as making a gift for a loved one or enhancing your living space. The emotional connection to the finished product enhances its value, imbuing it with memories and meaning that go beyond its functional use. This emotional investment creates a lasting bond with the project, making it a cherished part of your personal history.

Furthermore, DIY projects often create opportunities for social connection and community building. Sharing your progress and results with friends, family, or online communities can lead to valuable feedback, encouragement, and shared experiences. These interactions can deepen relationships and foster a sense of belonging, as you connect with others who share your interests and passions. Collaborating on projects or participating in DIY workshops and groups can also enhance these social benefits, creating a supportive network of like-minded individuals who inspire and motivate each other.

The environmental and economic benefits of DIY projects add another layer of satisfaction. By creating or repairing items yourself, you often reduce waste and promote sustainability. Upcycling materials, repurposing old items, and choosing eco-friendly options contribute to a more sustainable lifestyle. Additionally, DIY projects can be cost-effective, allowing you to save money or allocate resources more efficiently. The ability to create high-quality, custom items without relying on expensive commercial products can be financially rewarding, further enhancing the sense of accomplishment.

In essence, the accomplishment of a DIY project is a multifaceted experience that encompasses creativity, learning, empowerment, and personal fulfillment. It celebrates the joy of making, the satisfaction of overcoming challenges, and the pride of seeing a vision realized. Each project completed is a testament to your abilities, a tangible proof of your creativity and perseverance, and a source of ongoing joy and inspiration. The skills and confidence gained through DIY projects enrich your life, providing a foundation for future endeavors and a deeper appreciation for the art of creation. This journey of making is a celebration of human ingenuity and the enduring satisfaction of bringing something new and meaningful into the world.

Chapter 21: Creating Art for Pleasure

Creating art for pleasure is an endeavor that encompasses the joy of self-expression, the therapeutic benefits of engaging in creative activities, and the profound sense of fulfillment that comes from bringing one's inner visions to life. The act of creating art, whether through painting, drawing, sculpture, photography, or any other medium, is a deeply personal experience that allows individuals to explore and articulate their thoughts, emotions, and perceptions in a way that transcends words. This process of self-expression is inherently pleasurable, as it taps into the fundamental human drive to communicate and make sense of the world.

At the heart of creating art for pleasure is the joy of self-expression. Art provides a unique avenue for expressing ideas and emotions that might be difficult to convey through other means. The freedom to experiment with colors, shapes, forms, and textures allows for a limitless range of possibilities, each piece of art becoming a reflection of the artist's inner world. This creative freedom is immensely satisfying, as it allows individuals to explore their identities, beliefs, and experiences in a deeply personal and meaningful way. The process of translating intangible thoughts and feelings into tangible works of art can be both cathartic and exhilarating, providing a sense of release and accomplishment.

The therapeutic benefits of creating art are well-documented and widely recognized. Engaging in creative activities can serve as a powerful form of stress relief, offering a break from the demands and pressures of daily life. The act of focusing on a creative task can induce a state of flow, a mental state characterized by complete absorption and immersion in an activity. During this state, time seems to pass effortlessly, and worries and distractions fade into the background. This sense of flow is deeply pleasurable and can have significant mental health benefits, including reduced anxiety, improved mood, and enhanced overall well-being.

Art-making also provides a safe space for processing emotions and experiences. The creative process allows individuals to explore and express complex emotions in a non-verbal and non-judgmental way. For some, this can be a form of self-therapy, helping to work through difficult feelings or traumatic experiences. The act of creating something beautiful or meaningful out of pain or struggle can be empowering, fostering a sense of control and agency. Additionally, the physical act of making art, whether it involves drawing, painting, sculpting, or other techniques, can have a meditative quality, promoting relaxation and mindfulness.

The sense of fulfillment that comes from creating art is profound and multifaceted. Completing an artwork, no matter the scale or complexity, provides a tangible sense of accomplishment. This feeling of achievement is particularly gratifying because it results from one's own creativity and effort. The finished piece stands as a testament to the artist's skill, imagination, and perseverance. Displaying or sharing one's artwork can further enhance this sense of fulfillment, as it allows for the validation and appreciation of others. Positive feedback and recognition from friends, family, or the broader community can be incredibly rewarding and motivating, reinforcing the value and impact of one's creative efforts.

The pleasure of creating art also lies in the exploration and discovery that the creative process entails. Each new artwork is an opportunity to experiment with new techniques, styles, and ideas. This continuous learning and growth are inherently satisfying, as they challenge the artist to push their boundaries and expand their skills. The process of trial and error, while sometimes frustrating, is also a source of excitement and curiosity. Discovering new ways to express oneself, or finding unexpected solutions to creative challenges, can be incredibly rewarding. This spirit of exploration and innovation keeps the creative process dynamic and engaging, ensuring that the joy of creating art is ever-renewing.

Moreover, creating art for pleasure fosters a deep sense of connection, both to oneself and to others. The introspective nature of art-making encourages self-reflection and self-awareness, helping individuals to understand and articulate their inner experiences. This self-connection can be deeply fulfilling, as it nurtures a sense of authenticity and personal integrity. At the same time, art can be a powerful means of connecting with others. Sharing one's artwork can spark meaningful conversations and foster a sense of community and belonging. Art has the ability to transcend cultural and linguistic barriers, allowing for a shared appreciation of beauty, creativity, and human experience.

Creating art for pleasure also celebrates the beauty and diversity of the human experience. Art allows individuals to capture and highlight the unique aspects of their perspective, culture, and environment. This celebration of diversity enriches both the creator and the viewer, fostering a greater appreciation for the myriad ways in which humans perceive and interpret the world. The ability to create art that resonates with others, that evokes emotion or inspires thought, is a deeply gratifying experience. It reinforces the idea that art is a universal language, capable of communicating profound truths and fostering empathy and understanding.

The pleasure derived from creating art is not limited to the finished product but is deeply embedded in the process itself. The tactile experience of working with different materials, the visual delight of colors and forms coming together, and the intellectual challenge of solving creative problems all contribute to the joy of art-making. This multisensory engagement is both stimulating and soothing, providing a rich and immersive experience that can be enjoyed on many levels. Whether working in solitude or in a communal setting, the act of creating art is a source of continual pleasure and satisfaction.

In essence, creating art for pleasure is a deeply rewarding endeavor that nurtures the soul, stimulates the mind, and delights the senses. It is an exploration of self and an expression of individuality, a therapeutic practice, and a celebration of human creativity. The process of bringing a vision to life, of transforming raw materials into something meaningful and beautiful, is a source of profound joy and fulfillment. Each piece of art created is a testament to the artist's unique perspective and creative spirit, a lasting reminder of the pleasure and power of artistic expression.

Chapter 22: The Joy of Pet Companionship

The joy of pet companionship is a profound and multifaceted experience that enriches our lives in countless ways. Having a pet offers emotional support, companionship, and unconditional love, creating a bond that profoundly impacts our well-being and daily life. The presence of a pet can transform a house into a home, infusing it with warmth, vitality, and a sense of purpose. From dogs and cats to birds, rabbits, and even more exotic pets, the variety of animals that can become cherished companions is vast, each bringing unique qualities and joys into our lives.

One of the most significant aspects of pet companionship is the unconditional love and loyalty that pets provide. Unlike human relationships, which can be complex and conditional, the bond with a pet is straightforward and unwavering. Pets do not judge, hold grudges, or harbor expectations. They accept us as we are, flaws and all, offering a type of pure, unadulterated affection that is rare and precious. This unconditional love can be incredibly comforting, providing a stable source of emotional support, particularly during challenging times. Knowing that your pet is always there for you, ready to offer a wagging tail, a purr, or a nuzzle, can be a powerful antidote to stress, loneliness, and emotional turmoil.

The companionship provided by pets can significantly alleviate feelings of loneliness and isolation. In today's fast-paced world, where human interactions are often mediated by technology and social connections can be fleeting, the consistent presence of a pet can be profoundly grounding. Pets provide a sense of continuity and connection, anchoring us to the present moment and fostering a sense of belonging. For many people, especially those living alone or in isolated conditions, pets can be a lifeline, providing daily interaction, affection, and a reason to get up each day. The simple routines of pet care, such as feeding, walking, or grooming, create a sense of structure and purpose, helping to combat the aimlessness that can accompany loneliness.

Pets also offer a form of companionship that is deeply attuned to our emotional states. Many pets, particularly dogs and cats, are highly perceptive and responsive to their owners' moods and feelings. They can sense when we are sad, anxious, or unwell, often providing comfort and reassurance through their presence and behavior. A dog may lay its head on your lap when you are feeling down, or a cat might curl up beside you when you are stressed. This empathetic connection can be incredibly healing, providing a sense of being understood and cared for on a fundamental, non-verbal level.

The joy of pet companionship also extends to the physical benefits that come with pet ownership. Numerous studies have demonstrated that interacting with pets can lead to lower blood pressure, reduced stress levels, and improved cardiovascular health. The act of petting a dog or cat, for instance, has been shown to release oxytocin, a hormone associated with bonding and stress reduction, in both the pet and the owner. This physical interaction not only strengthens the bond between pet and owner but also promotes relaxation and well-being. Furthermore, the physical activity involved in caring for a pet, such as walking a dog or playing with a cat, encourages a more active lifestyle, which can have significant health benefits.

Pets also play a vital role in fostering social connections and community engagement. Walking a dog, for example, often leads to interactions with neighbors and other dog owners, facilitating social connections that might not otherwise occur. Pets can act as social catalysts, breaking down barriers and creating opportunities for conversation and shared experiences. For individuals who may find social interactions challenging, such as those with social anxiety or other conditions, pets can provide a bridge to more comfortable and meaningful social engagement. This aspect of pet companionship can greatly enhance one's social life and sense of community, contributing to overall happiness and well-being.

The joy of pet companionship is also reflected in the sense of purpose and responsibility that comes with caring for an animal. Pets rely on their owners for food, shelter, exercise, and affection, creating a mutual dependency that fosters a strong sense of purpose. The daily routines of pet care can provide structure and meaning, helping to organize one's day and prioritize responsibilities. This sense of purpose can be particularly beneficial for individuals struggling with depression, anxiety, or other mental health challenges, offering a consistent and meaningful focus that can help to anchor and stabilize one's life.

For children, growing up with pets can be especially rewarding and educational. Pets teach children about responsibility, empathy, and the importance of caring for others. The experience of feeding, grooming, and playing with a pet helps children develop a sense of accountability and compassion, fostering emotional and social development. Additionally, the companionship of a pet can provide children with comfort and security, acting as a trusted confidant and playmate. The bond between a child and a pet can be incredibly strong and formative, creating memories and lessons that last a lifetime.

The therapeutic benefits of pet companionship extend to various professional settings as well. Therapy animals, such as therapy dogs, are increasingly used in hospitals, nursing homes, and schools to provide comfort and support to patients, residents, and students. These animals can help to reduce anxiety, alleviate pain, and promote emotional healing in individuals facing various challenges. The presence of a therapy animal can create a more positive and comforting environment, enhancing the overall well-being of those they interact with. The use of therapy animals highlights the profound impact that pets can have on mental and emotional health, underscoring the value of pet companionship in diverse contexts.

The joy of pet companionship is also evident in the simple, everyday moments that pets bring into our lives. The playful antics of a kitten, the exuberant greeting of a dog when you come home, the soothing presence of a rabbit quietly munching on hay – these moments of joy and connection enrich our lives in countless ways. Pets have a unique ability to bring laughter, comfort, and a sense of wonder into our daily routines. They remind us of the beauty of the present moment, encouraging us to slow down, observe, and appreciate the simple pleasures of life.

Furthermore, the bond with a pet can inspire a deeper appreciation for nature and the environment. Caring for an animal often fosters a greater awareness of and connection to the natural world. Pet owners may become more attuned to the cycles of nature, such as the changing seasons and the needs of wildlife, as they care for their pets. This connection can inspire a more environmentally conscious lifestyle, encouraging behaviors that promote sustainability and the well-being of all living creatures.

In essence, the joy of pet companionship is a rich and multifaceted experience that touches upon nearly every aspect of our lives. It provides emotional support, physical health benefits, social connections, and a profound sense of purpose and fulfillment. The bond with a pet is a source of unconditional love, empathy, and joy, enriching our lives in ways that are both tangible and intangible. Pets teach us about responsibility, compassion, and the beauty of the present moment, offering a source of comfort and happiness that is truly unparalleled. The joy of pet companionship is a testament to the deep and enduring connection between humans and animals, a connection that continues to bring meaning, joy, and enrichment to our lives every day.

Chapter 23: Sharing Knowledge with Others

Sharing knowledge with others is a profoundly enriching endeavor that impacts individuals and communities on multiple levels. This practice encompasses the transmission of information, skills, and insights through various means, such as teaching, mentoring, collaborative projects, and casual conversations. The act of sharing knowledge is not only a cornerstone of education and professional development but also a vital component of personal growth and societal advancement. When we share knowledge, we contribute to a cycle of learning and improvement that benefits both the giver and the receiver, fostering a culture of continuous development and mutual support.

At the core of sharing knowledge is the desire to help others learn and grow. This altruistic impulse is driven by the recognition that knowledge is a powerful tool for empowerment and change. By imparting what we know to others, we enable them to navigate their challenges more effectively, make informed decisions, and pursue their goals with greater confidence. This empowerment is particularly significant in educational settings, where teachers and mentors play a crucial role in shaping the intellectual and personal development of their students. The knowledge shared in these contexts can open doors to new opportunities, inspire creativity, and instill a lifelong love of learning.

The process of sharing knowledge also reinforces and deepens our own understanding of the subject matter. Teaching others requires us to organize our thoughts, clarify complex concepts, and anticipate questions or misconceptions. This active engagement with the material helps to solidify our own knowledge and often leads to new insights and perspectives. The act of explaining a concept to someone else can reveal gaps in our understanding or highlight areas that need further exploration. This reciprocal relationship between teaching and learning underscores the idea that knowledge is not a finite resource but a dynamic and evolving entity that grows through interaction and exchange.

Sharing knowledge fosters a sense of community and collaboration. In professional and academic environments, knowledge sharing is essential for collective success and innovation. When individuals share their expertise and experiences, they contribute to a collective pool of knowledge that can be leveraged to solve problems, drive progress, and achieve common goals. This collaborative approach is particularly important in fields that rely on interdisciplinary knowledge and teamwork. By pooling resources and insights, teams can tackle complex challenges more effectively and develop innovative solutions that might not be possible through individual effort alone.

In addition to its practical benefits, sharing knowledge builds trust and strengthens relationships. When we share what we know with others, we demonstrate a willingness to invest in their growth and success. This act of generosity fosters goodwill and creates a positive, supportive environment. In workplaces, for instance, a culture of knowledge sharing can enhance team cohesion and morale, leading to increased productivity and job satisfaction. In personal relationships, sharing knowledge can deepen bonds and create a sense of shared purpose and understanding. The mutual exchange of ideas and experiences enriches our interactions and helps to build meaningful connections with others.

The impact of sharing knowledge extends beyond immediate relationships and environments. On a broader scale, it contributes to societal progress and innovation. Throughout history, the dissemination of knowledge has been a driving force behind major advancements in science, technology, culture, and governance. The spread of ideas through books, lectures, and, more recently, digital platforms has facilitated the exchange of information across geographical and cultural boundaries, leading to a more interconnected and informed world. In the digital age, the potential for knowledge sharing is greater than ever, with the internet providing unprecedented access to information and opportunities for global collaboration.

The democratization of knowledge through digital platforms has significant implications for education and equity. Online resources, such as open-access journals, educational websites, and virtual courses, have made high-quality knowledge more accessible to a wider audience. This increased access helps to bridge gaps in education and resources, providing opportunities for learning and development to individuals who might otherwise be excluded. The rise of online communities and social media has also facilitated peer-to-peer knowledge sharing, enabling people to connect, learn, and collaborate regardless of their location or background.

The practice of sharing knowledge is also closely linked to the development of critical thinking and problem-solving skills. Engaging with others in discussions and debates challenges us to consider different perspectives, question assumptions, and refine our arguments. This intellectual exchange stimulates creativity and innovation, as diverse viewpoints can lead to new ideas and approaches. In this way, knowledge sharing contributes to the development of a more thoughtful and informed society, where individuals are equipped to tackle complex issues and contribute to the common good.

Mentorship is a powerful form of knowledge sharing that has a profound impact on personal and professional development. Mentors provide guidance, support, and insights based on their own experiences and expertise, helping mentees navigate their career paths and achieve their goals. This relationship is mutually beneficial, as mentors also gain fresh perspectives and satisfaction from contributing to the growth of others. The transfer of knowledge and wisdom through mentorship fosters a culture of learning and leadership, ensuring that valuable skills and experiences are passed down to future generations.

Knowledge sharing can also play a crucial role in fostering cultural understanding and appreciation. By sharing knowledge about different cultures, traditions, and histories, we promote empathy and respect for diversity. This cultural exchange enriches our own understanding of the world and helps to build a more inclusive and harmonious society. Art, literature, music, and other forms of cultural expression are powerful mediums for sharing knowledge and experiences, providing insights into the values and perspectives of different communities.

In the context of professional development, knowledge sharing is essential for career growth and adaptability. The rapid pace of technological and industry changes requires continuous learning and skill development. By sharing knowledge and staying informed about new trends and developments, professionals can enhance their expertise and remain competitive in their fields. Knowledge sharing also promotes a culture of continuous improvement and innovation within organizations, driving progress and success.

In essence, sharing knowledge with others is a deeply enriching practice that benefits individuals, communities, and society as a whole. It empowers people to learn and grow, fosters collaboration and innovation, and builds trust and relationships. The act of sharing knowledge reinforces our own understanding and stimulates critical thinking and problem-solving. In a rapidly changing and interconnected world, the ability to share and disseminate knowledge is more important than ever, driving progress, equity, and cultural understanding. The joy and satisfaction derived from contributing to the growth and development of others are profound, highlighting the transformative power of knowledge sharing.

Chapter 24: Achieving a Personal Best

Achieving a personal best is a deeply fulfilling experience that reflects a significant milestone in an individual's journey towards self-improvement and mastery. This concept extends beyond mere performance metrics, encompassing the holistic growth of a person as they strive to surpass their own previous limits. Whether in sports, academics, professional endeavors, or personal hobbies, achieving a personal best is a testament to one's dedication, perseverance, and continuous effort. It involves setting goals, working diligently towards them, overcoming obstacles, and ultimately experiencing the profound satisfaction that comes from realizing one's full potential.

The journey towards achieving a personal best begins with setting clear, specific, and challenging goals. These goals provide direction and purpose, motivating individuals to push beyond their comfort zones and strive for excellence. Setting a goal that is both attainable and ambitious requires introspection and a realistic assessment of one's current abilities. It involves recognizing strengths and weaknesses and identifying areas for improvement. The process of goal-setting is empowering, as it transforms abstract aspirations into concrete targets, laying the groundwork for focused and deliberate action.

Once a goal is set, the path to achieving a personal best involves consistent and sustained effort. This commitment to improvement often requires the development of new skills, the refinement of existing abilities, and the adoption of disciplined practices. For an athlete, this might mean adhering to a rigorous training regimen, fine-tuning techniques, and maintaining peak physical condition. For a student, it could involve dedicated study, seeking out additional resources, and engaging in critical thinking. In a professional context, it might entail acquiring new knowledge, honing technical skills, and striving for excellence in one's field. Regardless of the specific domain, the pursuit of a personal best demands hard work, resilience, and a proactive approach to learning and growth.

One of the key components of achieving a personal best is overcoming obstacles and setbacks. The journey towards self-improvement is rarely linear or free from challenges. Individuals may encounter physical, mental, or emotional barriers that test their resolve and commitment. Injuries, failures, and disappointments are common hurdles that can impede progress. However, these challenges also present valuable opportunities for growth and learning. Overcoming adversity builds resilience and fortitude, teaching important lessons about perseverance and the power of a positive mindset. Each setback conquered strengthens the individual's character, enhancing their ability to tackle future challenges with confidence and determination.

The role of self-discipline and time management is crucial in achieving a personal best. Effective time management allows individuals to prioritize tasks, allocate resources efficiently, and maintain a balanced approach to their goals. Self-discipline involves resisting short-term temptations and distractions in favor of long-term benefits. It requires a strong sense of focus and the ability to stay committed to one's goals despite external pressures or internal doubts. Developing these qualities is essential for maintaining momentum and ensuring steady progress towards achieving a personal best.

Support and encouragement from others can also play a significant role in achieving a personal best. Mentors, coaches, family, and friends provide valuable guidance, feedback, and motivation. Their insights and perspectives can help individuals navigate challenges, refine their strategies, and stay inspired. The support of a community fosters a sense of belonging and accountability, creating a positive environment that encourages continuous improvement. Sharing the journey with others, celebrating milestones together, and receiving constructive feedback enhances the overall experience and reinforces the individual's commitment to their goals.

The psychological aspects of achieving a personal best are equally important. Positive self-talk, visualization, and goal-setting techniques can enhance motivation and performance. Believing in one's abilities and maintaining a positive attitude is crucial for overcoming self-doubt and anxiety. Visualization techniques, such as imagining successful outcomes and rehearsing positive scenarios, can build confidence and improve performance. Setting short-term, incremental goals provides a sense of achievement and keeps individuals motivated as they progress towards their ultimate objective. These psychological strategies create a mindset that is conducive to success, fostering a resilient and determined approach to achieving a personal best.

The sense of accomplishment that comes with achieving a personal best is profound and multifaceted. It is a reflection of the individual's hard work, dedication, and perseverance. The satisfaction derived from surpassing previous limits and realizing one's potential is deeply rewarding. This achievement boosts self-esteem and confidence, reinforcing the belief that greater heights can be reached with continued effort and determination. The experience of achieving a personal best often ignites a passion for further growth, inspiring individuals to set new goals and continue their pursuit of excellence.

Achieving a personal best also has a ripple effect, influencing various aspects of an individual's life. The skills and qualities developed during this journey, such as discipline, resilience, and time management, are transferable to other areas. The confidence and sense of accomplishment gained from achieving a personal best can enhance performance in professional and personal endeavors. It fosters a growth mindset, encouraging individuals to embrace challenges, seek continuous improvement, and view setbacks as opportunities for learning and development.

Moreover, achieving a personal best can inspire and motivate others. Sharing one's journey, challenges, and successes can have a positive impact on peers, colleagues, and the broader community. It demonstrates that with dedication, hard work, and perseverance, it is possible to overcome obstacles and achieve remarkable goals. This inspiration can create a culture of excellence and continuous improvement, where individuals support and encourage each other in their respective pursuits.

The journey towards achieving a personal best is also a celebration of the human spirit and its capacity for growth and transformation. It is a testament to the power of determination, the pursuit of excellence, and the unwavering belief in one's potential. This journey is not solely about the destination but also about the experiences, lessons, and growth encountered along the way. Each step taken, each challenge faced, and each milestone reached contributes to the individual's personal and professional development, creating a richer, more fulfilling life.

Chapter 25: The Gratitude of a Thank-You Note

The gratitude of a thank-you note is a nuanced and meaningful expression of appreciation that holds a timeless significance in human interactions. This simple act of writing a thank-you note transcends the boundaries of time and culture, embodying a genuine acknowledgment of kindness, generosity, and support. The impact of a well-crafted thank-you note extends far beyond its physical form, creating a lasting impression on both the sender and the recipient. It fosters a sense of connection, reinforces positive behaviors, and contributes to a culture of gratitude and respect. Delving into the intricate aspects of thank-you notes reveals their profound emotional, social, and psychological dimensions, underscoring their importance in personal and professional relationships.

At its core, a thank-you note is a tangible manifestation of gratitude. It goes beyond verbal expressions of thanks by providing a written record that can be revisited and cherished. The process of writing a thank-you note involves thoughtful reflection on the recipient's actions and the impact they had on the sender. This reflection fosters a deeper understanding and appreciation of the kindness or generosity received. The act of putting pen to paper requires the sender to articulate their feelings clearly and sincerely, enhancing the authenticity and depth of the expression. This level of effort and consideration adds a personal touch that is often lost in fleeting verbal exchanges or digital messages.

The emotional impact of receiving a thank-you note is significant. For the recipient, it serves as a heartfelt acknowledgment of their actions and the positive effect they had on someone else. This recognition can evoke feelings of validation, satisfaction, and happiness. It reinforces the idea that their efforts were noticed and appreciated, which can be particularly meaningful in situations where the recipient may not have expected any recognition. In a professional context, a thank-you note can boost morale and motivation, affirming that their contributions are valued and making them feel more connected to their work and colleagues. In personal relationships, a thank-you note can strengthen bonds and enhance mutual respect and affection.

The social dimension of thank-you notes is equally important. They play a crucial role in maintaining and nurturing relationships by fostering a sense of reciprocity and goodwill. A thank-you note acknowledges the interdependence between individuals and reinforces social norms of courtesy and respect. It demonstrates that the sender values the relationship and is willing to invest time and effort in expressing their gratitude. This gesture can deepen existing connections and lay the foundation for future interactions, creating a positive feedback loop of kindness and appreciation. In professional settings, thank-you notes can enhance networking efforts, leaving a positive impression and opening doors to new opportunities and collaborations.

The psychological benefits of expressing gratitude through thank-you notes are well-documented. Research has shown that practicing gratitude can lead to increased well-being, improved mental health, and greater life satisfaction. Writing a thank-you note encourages individuals to focus on the positive aspects of their experiences and the people who have contributed to their happiness and success. This shift in focus can reduce stress, foster a more optimistic outlook, and enhance overall emotional resilience. The act of expressing gratitude also cultivates a sense of mindfulness and presence, as individuals take the time to reflect on and appreciate the kindness they have received.

Crafting a thank-you note involves several key elements that contribute to its effectiveness and impact. The content should be specific, highlighting the particular actions or qualities for which the sender is grateful. This specificity not only makes the note more personal and meaningful but also demonstrates that the sender has taken the time to reflect on and truly appreciate the recipient's efforts. Additionally, the tone of the note should be warm and sincere, conveying genuine feelings of gratitude and appreciation. The use of positive language and expressions of hope for future interactions can further enhance the note's impact, leaving the recipient with a lasting sense of goodwill.

The physical form of a thank-you note also adds to its significance. In an age dominated by digital communication, a handwritten note stands out as a rare and cherished artifact. The tactile nature of paper and ink adds a personal and enduring quality to the message, making it something that can be kept and treasured. The choice of stationery, the handwriting, and even the act of sealing and delivering the note all contribute to its overall impact. These tangible elements create a sensory experience that reinforces the emotional content of the message, making the expression of gratitude more memorable and meaningful.

Thank-you notes also serve as powerful tools for personal and professional development. They encourage individuals to practice empathy, as they must consider the perspective and feelings of the recipient when crafting their message. This practice of empathy can enhance interpersonal skills and foster a greater understanding of others. In a professional context, writing thank-you notes can improve communication skills and demonstrate a high level of professionalism and courtesy. This habit of expressing gratitude can also contribute to a positive reputation, as individuals who consistently acknowledge and appreciate the efforts of others are often perceived as more likable and trustworthy.

The act of writing a thank-you note can be particularly meaningful in moments of significant personal or professional milestones.

Whether it's acknowledging a mentor's guidance during a career transition, expressing thanks for a friend's support during a difficult time, or recognizing a colleague's help on a challenging project, thank-you notes capture the essence of these pivotal moments. They serve as a record of gratitude and appreciation that can be looked back on with fondness, reminding both the sender and the recipient of the positive impact they had on each other's lives.

Thank-you notes also play an essential role in cultural and social rituals, marking important events and transitions. In many cultures, thank-you notes are an integral part of celebrations such as weddings, birthdays, and holidays. They offer a formal and heartfelt way to acknowledge gifts, support, and well-wishes received during these special occasions. This tradition of expressing gratitude helps to strengthen social bonds and maintain a sense of community and connection. In professional contexts, thank-you notes are often used to follow up on job interviews, client meetings, and business transactions, reinforcing professional relationships and demonstrating a commitment to courteous and respectful communication.

The practice of writing thank-you notes can be adapted to modern contexts while preserving its essential qualities. Digital thank-you notes, for example, can be crafted with the same level of care and sincerity as handwritten ones. Personalized emails, e-cards, and messages on social media platforms can effectively convey gratitude in a format that suits today's fast-paced communication landscape. While the tactile experience may be different, the underlying principles of specificity, sincerity, and personal connection remain the same. These digital expressions of gratitude can reach recipients quickly and conveniently, ensuring that the timely acknowledgment of kindness and support.

Ultimately, the gratitude of a thank-you note lies in its ability to capture and convey the essence of appreciation and acknowledgment. It transforms a simple expression of thanks into a meaningful and lasting gesture that resonates with both the sender and the recipient. The act of writing a thank-you note is a powerful reminder of the importance of gratitude in our lives, encouraging us to recognize and celebrate the positive contributions of others. It fosters a culture of appreciation and respect, enhances personal and professional relationships, and contributes to a sense of well-being and fulfillment. In a world where genuine expressions of gratitude can sometimes be overlooked, the humble thank-you note remains a timeless and invaluable practice that enriches our lives and strengthens our connections with others.

Chapter 26: Practicing Mindfulness Daily

Practicing mindfulness daily is a profound and transformative practice that can significantly enhance one's overall well-being and quality of life. Mindfulness, rooted in ancient meditative traditions, involves paying full attention to the present moment with openness, curiosity, and without judgment. By cultivating this awareness, individuals can develop a deeper understanding of their thoughts, emotions, and physical sensations, leading to greater emotional resilience, improved mental health, and a more fulfilling life. Delving into the various dimensions of daily mindfulness practice reveals its extensive benefits, techniques, and the challenges that come with integrating it into everyday life.

At its core, mindfulness is about being fully present and engaged in the current moment. This can be achieved through various practices such as meditation, mindful breathing, body scans, and mindful walking. Each of these practices helps to anchor the mind in the present, allowing individuals to observe their thoughts and feelings without getting caught up in them. This non-reactive awareness helps to create a space between stimulus and response, providing an opportunity to choose more thoughtful and constructive reactions.

One of the fundamental benefits of practicing mindfulness daily is its positive impact on mental health. Regular mindfulness practice has been shown to reduce symptoms of anxiety, depression, and stress. By fostering a greater awareness of the present moment, mindfulness helps individuals to break free from the cycle of negative thinking patterns that often contribute to these mental health issues. For instance, by observing thoughts and feelings as they arise without judgment, individuals can prevent themselves from being overwhelmed by them, thereby reducing their emotional impact. This ability to maintain a balanced and non-reactive mindset can be particularly beneficial in managing stress and preventing burnout.

Mindfulness also plays a crucial role in enhancing emotional regulation. By practicing mindfulness, individuals can develop a better understanding of their emotional responses and learn to manage them more effectively. This involves recognizing and acknowledging emotions without suppressing or reacting to them impulsively. Over time, this practice helps to build emotional resilience, enabling individuals to cope with difficult situations and emotions with greater ease. This enhanced emotional regulation can lead to improved relationships, better decision-making, and a more balanced and harmonious life.

In addition to its mental health benefits, mindfulness can also improve physical health. Regular mindfulness practice has been associated with lower blood pressure, improved immune function, and reduced inflammation. These physical health benefits are likely due to the stress-reducing effects of mindfulness, as chronic stress is known to have a detrimental impact on the body. By reducing stress levels and promoting relaxation, mindfulness can help to prevent a range of stress-related health issues, including cardiovascular disease, chronic pain, and gastrointestinal problems.

One of the key aspects of practicing mindfulness daily is developing a routine that incorporates mindfulness into various activities throughout the day. This can involve setting aside specific times for formal mindfulness practices, such as meditation or mindful breathing exercises. For example, starting the day with a few minutes of mindful breathing can set a positive tone for the day ahead, helping to cultivate a sense of calm and focus. Similarly, incorporating mindfulness into daily activities, such as eating, walking, or even washing dishes, can help to maintain a state of present-moment awareness throughout the day. These informal practices provide opportunities to practice mindfulness in a variety of contexts, making it easier to integrate into daily life.

Mindful breathing is one of the most accessible and effective mindfulness practices. It involves focusing attention on the breath as it flows in and out of the body, observing the sensations associated with each inhale and exhale. This practice helps to anchor the mind in the present moment and can be particularly useful during times of stress or anxiety. By paying attention to the breath, individuals can create a sense of calm and stability, which can help to reduce the intensity of negative emotions and promote relaxation.

Body scan meditation is another powerful mindfulness practice that involves systematically focusing attention on different parts of the body, observing any sensations without judgment. This practice helps to cultivate a greater awareness of the body and can be particularly effective in reducing physical tension and promoting relaxation. By paying attention to bodily sensations, individuals can develop a deeper connection with their physical self, which can help to enhance overall well-being and reduce the impact of stress on the body.

Mindful walking is a practice that involves bringing awareness to the act of walking, paying attention to the sensations of the feet touching the ground, the movement of the legs, and the rhythm of the breath. This practice can be done anywhere, whether walking in nature, in the city, or even indoors. Mindful walking helps to integrate mindfulness into daily life and can be a powerful way to cultivate present-moment awareness while staying active.

Another important aspect of practicing mindfulness daily is cultivating a mindful attitude towards thoughts and emotions. This involves observing thoughts and emotions as they arise without getting caught up in them or reacting to them impulsively. By adopting a non-judgmental and curious attitude, individuals can develop a greater understanding of their inner experiences and learn to respond to them in a more constructive and balanced way. This practice can help to break the cycle of negative thinking patterns and promote a more positive and resilient mindset.

In addition to these formal practices, incorporating mindfulness into everyday activities can be a powerful way to cultivate present-moment awareness throughout the day. For example, practicing mindful eating involves paying full attention to the experience of eating, savoring each bite, and noticing the flavors, textures, and sensations associated with the food. This practice can help to develop a greater appreciation for food, promote healthier eating habits, and enhance overall well-being. Similarly, practicing mindfulness while engaging in daily chores, such as cleaning or cooking, can transform these activities into opportunities for mindfulness practice, helping to maintain a state of present-moment awareness throughout the day.

Despite the many benefits of practicing mindfulness daily, integrating it into daily life can be challenging. One of the common obstacles is finding the time to practice mindfulness regularly. In today's fast-paced world, it can be difficult to set aside time for mindfulness practice amidst the demands of work, family, and other responsibilities. However, it is important to remember that mindfulness can be practiced in short, manageable sessions, and even a few minutes of mindfulness practice each day can have a significant impact on overall well-being. By making mindfulness a priority and incorporating it into daily routines, individuals can create a sustainable and meaningful mindfulness practice.

Another challenge is maintaining a consistent mindfulness practice. It is common to experience fluctuations in motivation and commitment, especially during times of stress or when faced with other distractions. To maintain a consistent practice, it can be helpful to set realistic goals and establish a routine that incorporates mindfulness into daily activities. Additionally, finding a supportive community or mindfulness group can provide encouragement and accountability, making it easier to stay committed to the practice.

Mindfulness is not a quick fix or a one-size-fits-all solution. It is a skill that requires ongoing practice and commitment. There may be times when mindfulness practice feels challenging or even uncomfortable, especially when confronting difficult thoughts or emotions. However, it is important to approach these experiences with a non-judgmental and compassionate attitude, recognizing that mindfulness is a journey of self-discovery and growth. By persevering through challenges and maintaining a regular practice, individuals can experience the profound and transformative benefits of mindfulness.

Chapter 27: The Triumph of Problem-Solving

The triumph of problem-solving is a fundamental aspect of human experience that permeates various aspects of our lives. From personal challenges to professional dilemmas, the ability to navigate and resolve problems is a skill that underpins success and progress. This intricate process involves critical thinking, creativity, persistence, and the application of knowledge and skills. The sense of accomplishment that comes from overcoming obstacles and finding solutions is deeply rewarding, fostering personal growth, innovation, and a deeper understanding of the world around us. Exploring the multifaceted nature of problem-solving reveals its profound impact on individuals and society as a whole.

At its core, problem-solving is the process of identifying a problem, analyzing its components, and devising and implementing strategies to overcome it. This process begins with problem identification, which involves recognizing that a problem exists and defining its nature and scope. Clear problem identification is crucial, as it sets the stage for effective analysis and solution generation. This step often requires critical observation and analytical thinking to understand the underlying causes and implications of the problem. Accurate problem identification can prevent misdirected efforts and ensure that resources are focused on addressing the actual issue.

Once a problem is identified, the next step is to analyze it thoroughly. This involves breaking the problem down into smaller, more manageable parts and examining each component to understand its role in the overall issue. Analytical thinking is key during this stage, as it allows individuals to uncover patterns, relationships, and root causes that may not be immediately apparent. Tools such as SWOT analysis (Strengths, Weaknesses, Opportunities, Threats), root cause analysis, and brainstorming sessions can aid in this process. A comprehensive analysis provides a solid foundation for generating potential solutions, as it highlights the key factors that need to be addressed.

Creativity plays a vital role in the problem-solving process, particularly during the solution-generation phase. Creative thinking involves looking beyond conventional approaches and exploring innovative ideas and perspectives. This can lead to the discovery of novel solutions that may not have been considered through traditional problem-solving methods. Techniques such as lateral thinking, mind mapping, and brainstorming can foster creative thinking and encourage the exploration of a wide range of potential solutions. Encouraging creativity in problem-solving can lead to breakthroughs and advancements that drive progress and innovation in various fields.

The implementation of solutions is another critical aspect of problem-solving. This involves developing a detailed plan of action, allocating resources, and executing the chosen solution. Effective implementation requires careful planning, coordination, and monitoring to ensure that the solution is carried out as intended. It is also important to remain flexible and adaptable, as unforeseen challenges and obstacles may arise during the implementation process. Continuous evaluation and feedback can help to identify any issues and make necessary adjustments to ensure the success of the solution.

Persistence and resilience are essential qualities in problem-solving. Not all problems can be solved quickly or easily, and setbacks and failures are a natural part of the process. The ability to persevere in the face of challenges and maintain a positive and determined mindset is crucial for overcoming obstacles and finding effective solutions. Resilience involves learning from failures and setbacks, using them as opportunities for growth and improvement. This mindset can help individuals to stay motivated and focused, even when the problem-solving process becomes difficult or frustrating.

The triumph of problem-solving extends beyond the individual level to have a significant impact on teams, organizations, and society as a whole. In a team or organizational context, effective problem-solving can lead to improved performance, increased efficiency, and greater innovation. Collaborative problem-solving involves leveraging the diverse skills, knowledge, and perspectives of team members to generate and implement solutions. This collaborative approach can lead to more comprehensive and effective solutions, as well as fostering a sense of teamwork and shared accomplishment.

In the broader context of society, problem-solving drives progress and development. Throughout history, human ingenuity and problem-solving abilities have led to remarkable advancements in science, technology, medicine, and various other fields. From the invention of the wheel to the development of the internet, the ability to identify and solve problems has been a key driver of human civilization. Addressing complex societal issues such as poverty, climate change, and healthcare requires innovative and collaborative problem-solving efforts. By applying critical thinking, creativity, and persistence, individuals and organizations can contribute to meaningful solutions that benefit society as a whole.

The psychological and emotional rewards of problem-solving are also significant. Successfully solving a problem can lead to a sense of accomplishment, satisfaction, and increased self-efficacy. This positive reinforcement can boost confidence and motivation, encouraging individuals to tackle new challenges and continue developing their problem-solving skills. The process of solving problems also promotes personal growth and learning, as individuals gain new knowledge, skills, and insights through their experiences. This continuous learning and development can enhance overall well-being and contribute to a fulfilling and purposeful life.

Problem-solving also plays a crucial role in personal relationships and daily life. From resolving conflicts and making decisions to managing time and resources, the ability to solve problems effectively is essential for maintaining healthy and balanced relationships. Effective communication, empathy, and negotiation skills are important components of interpersonal problem-solving, as they enable individuals to understand and address the needs and perspectives of others. In daily life, problem-solving skills can help individuals to navigate challenges, make informed decisions, and achieve their personal goals.

The development of problem-solving skills can be nurtured and enhanced through education and practice. Educational programs that emphasize critical thinking, creativity, and collaborative problem-solving can equip individuals with the tools and skills needed to tackle complex problems. Practical experiences, such as hands-on projects, case studies, and real-world problem-solving scenarios, can provide valuable opportunities for individuals to apply and refine their problem-solving abilities. Continuous learning and practice are essential for developing and maintaining strong problem-solving skills, as they enable individuals to adapt to new challenges and environments.

Chapter 28: Celebrating Creative Writing

Celebrating creative writing is a multifaceted and enriching endeavor that honors the power of imagination, the beauty of language, and the profound impact of storytelling. Creative writing encompasses a wide range of genres and forms, including poetry, fiction, drama, and creative nonfiction. Each of these forms offers unique opportunities for self-expression, exploration of ideas, and connection with readers. The celebration of creative writing involves recognizing and appreciating the skill, effort, and creativity that writers bring to their work, as well as understanding the cultural and personal significance of written expression. Delving deeply into the various aspects of creative writing reveals its transformative power and the reasons it deserves to be celebrated.

At its core, creative writing is a form of artistic expression that allows writers to explore and convey their thoughts, emotions, and experiences through the written word. It is a process that involves imagination, inspiration, and technical skill. The act of writing creatively enables individuals to transcend the boundaries of their everyday lives, transporting them to new worlds, different times, and alternative realities. This imaginative journey is not only exhilarating for the writer but also for the reader, who is invited to embark on a shared adventure through the pages of a story or poem.

One of the primary reasons to celebrate creative writing is its capacity to evoke emotions and provoke thought. Through carefully crafted language and vivid imagery, writers can create powerful emotional experiences for their readers. A well-written story or poem can elicit a wide range of emotions, from joy and excitement to sorrow and contemplation. This emotional resonance is a testament to the writer's ability to connect with their audience on a deep and meaningful level. By evoking empathy and understanding, creative writing can foster a greater sense of shared humanity and compassion.

Creative writing also has the power to illuminate the human experience in ways that are both profound and relatable. Writers often draw inspiration from their own lives, as well as from the lives of others, to create stories and characters that reflect the complexities of the human condition. This exploration of themes such as love, loss, identity, and resilience allow readers to see themselves and their own experiences mirrored in the narrative. Through this reflection, readers can gain new insights and perspectives, as well as a greater appreciation for the diversity and richness of human life.

Another significant aspect of celebrating creative writing is recognizing its role in preserving and sharing cultural heritage. Stories, poems, and plays have long been used to pass down traditions, beliefs, and values from one generation to the next. By capturing the essence of a particular culture or community, creative writing helps to preserve its history and identity. This cultural preservation is essential for maintaining a sense of continuity and connection, especially in a rapidly changing world. Additionally, creative writing provides a platform for marginalized voices and underrepresented communities to share their stories and experiences, contributing to a more inclusive and equitable literary landscape.

The celebration of creative writing also involves acknowledging the skill and craftsmanship that writers bring to their work. Writing creatively is not simply about putting words on paper; it is a meticulous and intentional process that requires a deep understanding of language, structure, and form. Writers must hone their technical skills, such as grammar, syntax, and punctuation, while also mastering elements of storytelling, such as character development, plot, and pacing. This combination of technical proficiency and artistic vision is what allows writers to create compelling and impactful works of literature.

In addition to technical skill, creativity is at the heart of the writing process. Creativity involves thinking outside the box, taking risks, and pushing the boundaries of conventional storytelling. Writers often experiment with different narrative techniques, perspectives, and styles to create unique and original works. This willingness to innovate and explore new possibilities is what keeps the literary world vibrant and dynamic. Celebrating creative writing means celebrating the endless potential of the human imagination and the ability to bring new and exciting ideas to life through words.

The journey of writing creatively is also a deeply personal and transformative one. For many writers, the act of writing is a form of self-discovery and self-expression. It provides an outlet for exploring their inner world, processing emotions, and making sense of their experiences. This introspective journey can lead to personal growth and healing, as writers gain a greater understanding of themselves and their place in the world. By sharing their personal stories and insights, writers can also inspire and resonate with readers who may be going through similar experiences.

The communal aspect of creative writing is another reason to celebrate it. Writing is often seen as a solitary activity, but it also has the power to bring people together. Writers' groups, literary festivals, and writing workshops provide opportunities for writers to connect, share their work, and receive feedback and support from their peers. These communities foster a sense of camaraderie and mutual encouragement, helping writers to grow and thrive. Additionally, the act of reading and discussing literature creates a shared experience that can bridge gaps and build connections between people from different backgrounds and walks of life.

The impact of creative writing extends beyond the individual and the community to society as a whole. Literature has the power to challenge societal norms, question injustices, and spark social change. Through their work, writers can shine a light on important issues, raise awareness, and inspire action. Whether it is through a novel that addresses systemic racism, a poem that explores gender identity, or a play that critiques political corruption, creative writing can be a powerful tool for advocacy and activism. Celebrating creative writing means recognizing its potential to contribute to a more just and equitable world.

In an educational context, creative writing plays a vital role in developing critical thinking, communication, and empathy skills. Encouraging students to write creatively allows them to explore their ideas and emotions, think critically about the world around them, and articulate their thoughts clearly and effectively. Creative writing also fosters a love of reading and literature, which can have a lasting impact on students' academic and personal lives. By celebrating creative writing in schools and universities, educators can cultivate a new generation of thinkers, writers, and readers who are equipped to engage with and contribute to the world in meaningful ways.

The celebration of creative writing is also an acknowledgment of the diverse voices and stories that enrich our literary landscape. The literary world has historically been dominated by certain voices, but there is a growing recognition of the importance of diversity and inclusion in literature. Celebrating creative writing means uplifting and amplifying the voices of writers from different backgrounds, cultures, and perspectives. This diversity not only enriches the literary canon but also provides readers with a broader and more inclusive understanding of the world.

In the digital age, the landscape of creative writing is continually evolving. The rise of digital platforms and social media has democratized the publishing process, allowing more writers to share their work with a global audience. This accessibility has led to an explosion of creativity and innovation in the literary world. Online communities, blogs, and self-publishing platforms provide new opportunities for writers to connect with readers and build their careers. Celebrating creative writing means embracing these new possibilities and recognizing the ways in which technology is transforming the literary landscape.

Lastly, the celebration of creative writing is an appreciation of the joy and pleasure that it brings to both writers and readers. There is a unique and profound joy in the act of creating something new, of bringing characters and stories to life, and of playing with language and form. For readers, there is the delight of discovering new worlds, becoming immersed in compelling narratives, and experiencing the beauty of well-crafted prose and poetry. This shared joy is what makes creative writing such a powerful and enduring form of expression.

Chapter 29: The Serenity of a Nature Walk

The serenity of a nature walk is an experience that transcends the simple act of walking through natural surroundings. It encompasses the tranquility and peace that envelop the mind and body, offering a reprieve from the hustle and bustle of daily life. Engaging with nature in this way has profound psychological, emotional, and physical benefits, fostering a deep sense of connection to the natural world. The practice of taking a nature walk can be seen as a form of moving meditation, where the rhythmic pace of walking harmonizes with the sights, sounds, and smells of the natural environment, creating a holistic and rejuvenating experience.

One of the primary aspects of the serenity found in a nature walk is the sensory immersion it provides. Unlike urban environments filled with artificial stimuli, nature offers a tapestry of organic sights, sounds, and smells that can soothe the mind and body. The rustling of leaves, the chirping of birds, the sight of sunlight filtering through the canopy, and the scent of fresh earth and blooming flowers all contribute to a multi-sensory experience that calms and invigorates. This sensory richness helps to ground individuals in the present moment, making it easier to let go of worries and stressors that may have accumulated throughout the day.

The physical act of walking itself plays a crucial role in fostering serenity. Walking is a natural, rhythmic activity that promotes physical health by improving cardiovascular function, enhancing muscle tone, and boosting overall stamina. When combined with the fresh air and varied terrain of a natural setting, these benefits are amplified. The gentle exercise of a nature walk helps to release endorphins, which are the body's natural mood enhancers, leading to feelings of well-being and happiness. Moreover, the physical activity involved in walking can help to reduce the levels of cortisol, the stress hormone, thereby promoting a state of relaxation and calm.

The mental health benefits of a nature walk are profound and well-documented. Numerous studies have shown that spending time in nature can reduce symptoms of anxiety, depression, and stress. The natural environment provides a stark contrast to the often overwhelming and hectic urban lifestyle, offering a space where individuals can slow down and reconnect with themselves. The concept of "forest bathing," or Shinrin-yoku, which originated in Japan, encapsulates this idea. It involves immersing oneself in a forest setting to absorb its calming and restorative effects. This practice has been scientifically proven to lower blood pressure, reduce cortisol levels, and enhance overall mental well-being.

A nature walk also fosters a sense of mindfulness, which is the practice of being fully present and engaged in the current moment. As one walks through a forest, along a beach, or across a meadow, there are countless opportunities to practice mindfulness. The rhythmic crunch of leaves underfoot, the feel of a gentle breeze on the skin, and the intricate details of a flower or a leaf all serve as focal points for mindfulness practice. By paying close attention to these details, individuals can cultivate a deeper awareness of their surroundings and their own internal states, leading to a greater sense of peace and contentment.

The spiritual aspect of a nature walk should not be overlooked. For many people, spending time in nature is a deeply spiritual experience that fosters a sense of connection to something greater than themselves. This connection can be to the natural world, to the universe, or to a higher power, depending on one's beliefs. The vastness and beauty of nature can evoke feelings of awe and wonder, prompting introspection and a reevaluation of one's place in the world. This spiritual dimension of a nature walk can lead to profound insights and a renewed sense of purpose and meaning in life.

Moreover, the solitude often found on a nature walk can be both comforting and enlightening. In the stillness of nature, away from the constant demands and distractions of modern life, individuals have the opportunity to reflect and reconnect with their innermost thoughts and feelings. This solitude can foster a sense of self-discovery and personal growth, as well as providing a space for problem-solving and creative thinking. The quietude of a nature walk allows the mind to wander freely, often leading to unexpected insights and solutions to problems that may have seemed insurmountable in a more hectic environment.

The social dimension of a nature walk can also contribute to its serenity. While solitary walks offer profound benefits, walking with others can enhance the experience through shared enjoyment and connection. Engaging in conversation with a friend or family member while surrounded by nature can deepen relationships and create lasting memories. The shared experience of witnessing a beautiful sunset, encountering wildlife, or simply enjoying the peace of the natural setting can strengthen bonds and foster a sense of community and belonging.

The impact of a nature walk extends beyond the immediate experience, offering lasting benefits that can enhance overall quality of life. Regular engagement with nature can lead to sustained improvements in mental and physical health, greater emotional resilience, and a more positive outlook on life. The practice of taking nature walks can become a cherished routine that individuals look forward to, providing a consistent source of joy and relaxation. This ongoing relationship with nature can inspire a greater appreciation for the natural world and a commitment to its preservation and stewardship.

The educational aspect of a nature walk is another important facet to consider. Nature provides a living classroom where individuals can learn about the intricate web of life, ecological processes, and the interdependence of species. Observing the behaviors of animals, the growth patterns of plants, and the changing seasons can deepen one's understanding of and respect for the natural world. This knowledge can foster a sense of environmental responsibility and a desire to protect and conserve natural habitats for future generations.

Chapter 30: Reconnecting with Old Friends

Reconnecting with old friends is a deeply enriching and profoundly significant experience that touches upon the essence of human relationships and the enduring nature of true friendship. It involves rekindling bonds that may have been temporarily set aside due to the various demands and changes in our lives. The act of reaching out to and reconnecting with friends from our past is often filled with nostalgia, reflection, and a sense of rediscovery. It allows individuals to revisit shared memories, appreciate personal growth, and reaffirm the meaningful connections that have shaped their lives. This process is not only about reestablishing contact but also about celebrating the history, trust, and understanding that exist within these cherished relationships.

The journey of reconnecting with old friends often begins with a sense of longing or curiosity. As people navigate through different phases of life—such as moving to new places, pursuing careers, or starting families—it is natural for some friendships to become distant. This distance, however, does not necessarily signify the end of a relationship but rather a pause in its active chapter. The urge to reconnect might be sparked by a significant life event, a random memory, or simply the realization that an important person from the past is missed. This initial spark serves as a powerful motivator to reach out and bridge the gap that time and circumstances may have created.

The act of reaching out to an old friend can be both exciting and nerve-wracking. It requires a certain level of vulnerability and courage, as there is always the uncertainty of how the other person will respond. Will they be receptive? Will they remember the friendship as fondly? These questions can create apprehension, but they also underscore the value placed on the relationship. When an old friend responds positively, it validates the shared bond and opens the door to a renewed connection. This initial communication, whether it's a message, a phone call, or a letter, sets the stage for a deeper reconnection.

One of the most rewarding aspects of reconnecting with old friends is the opportunity to reminisce and share memories. Revisiting past experiences, both joyful and challenging, strengthens the sense of camaraderie and shared history. These memories often include pivotal moments such as school days, adventures, milestones, and even the mundane yet meaningful everyday interactions. Reflecting on these experiences can bring about a sense of nostalgia, a bittersweet recognition of time passed, and a deep appreciation for the enduring nature of the friendship. The act of reminiscing is not just about looking back; it is also about acknowledging how those experiences have contributed to personal growth and the person one has become.

Another important facet of reconnecting with old friends is the mutual exchange of life updates. Catching up on each other's journeys since the last time they were in close contact can be a profound experience. This exchange includes sharing achievements, challenges, changes, and aspirations. Learning about each other's paths provides a deeper understanding and often leads to a renewed sense of admiration and respect. It is fascinating to see how each person has navigated their own life, and these updates can sometimes reveal surprising parallels or contrasting experiences that enrich the conversation and strengthen the bond.

Reconnecting with old friends also provides an opportunity to heal past misunderstandings or unresolved issues. Time and distance can offer new perspectives, allowing individuals to approach old conflicts with greater empathy and understanding. This aspect of reconnection can be incredibly healing, as it offers a chance for closure and reconciliation. Addressing and resolving past issues can remove lingering negative emotions and pave the way for a healthier, more positive relationship moving forward. It is a testament to the strength and resilience of the friendship that it can withstand and grow from such honest and vulnerable conversations.

The rekindling of old friendships can lead to the rediscovery of shared interests and values. While individuals grow and change over time, core interests and values often remain. This common ground serves as a foundation for renewed connections and shared activities. Engaging in familiar hobbies, exploring new interests together, or simply spending time in each other's company can recreate the camaraderie and joy of the past while adding new dimensions to the friendship. This shared time is not just a return to the old ways but also an evolution of the relationship, integrating past bonds with present realities.

Reconnecting with old friends can also introduce new perspectives and insights into one's life. Old friends often know us in ways that new acquaintances may not. They have seen us through different stages of life and can offer unique reflections on our growth and character. Their insights can be invaluable, providing clarity and encouragement. Moreover, the exchange of experiences and wisdom gained over the years can be mutually beneficial, offering new ways of thinking and understanding the world. This dynamic exchange enriches both individuals, fostering a deeper connection and a sense of mutual support.

The emotional support and validation that come from reconnecting with old friends cannot be overstated. These friends often understand our history, context, and the nuances of our experiences. This understanding creates a safe space where individuals can express their thoughts and feelings without fear of judgment. The emotional support provided by old friends is rooted in a deep-seated trust and familiarity, making it particularly comforting and reassuring. This support can be especially valuable during challenging times, as it comes from a place of genuine care and long-standing connection.

Reconnecting with old friends also highlights the importance of maintaining and nurturing relationships. It serves as a reminder that meaningful connections require effort and intentionality. While life's demands can make it easy to drift apart, the act of reaching out and reconnecting underscores the value placed on the friendship. This awareness can inspire individuals to prioritize their relationships, making time for regular communication and shared activities. Nurturing these connections enhances the quality of life, providing a network of support, joy, and companionship.

In the broader context, reconnecting with old friends can contribute to a sense of continuity and belonging. It ties the past to the present, creating a cohesive narrative of one's life. This continuity is comforting, as it affirms that despite the changes and transitions, certain relationships remain constant. The sense of belonging that comes from reconnecting with old friends can also enhance one's overall well-being. It reinforces the idea that we are part of a larger tapestry of relationships and experiences, providing a sense of stability and rootedness.

The celebration of milestones and achievements is another rewarding aspect of reconnecting with old friends. Whether it's personal milestones like birthdays, anniversaries, or professional achievements, old friends who have witnessed our journey can share in these celebrations with genuine joy and pride. Their acknowledgment and celebration of our achievements add a layer of meaning and significance. Similarly, being able to celebrate their milestones strengthens the bond and creates new shared memories that enhance the relationship.

In the digital age, the process of reconnecting with old friends has been made more accessible through social media and communication technology. Platforms like Facebook, Instagram, and LinkedIn allow individuals to find and reconnect with friends from different phases of their lives. These tools facilitate initial contact and make it easier to stay in touch, even across long distances. However, while digital communication is a valuable tool, the quality of the reconnection often benefits from more personal interactions, such as phone calls, video chats, or in-person meetings. These interactions add depth and authenticity to the reconnection process.

Chapter 31: The Confidence of Public Speaking

The confidence of public speaking is a multifaceted skill that plays a critical role in personal and professional development. Public speaking is the act of delivering a speech or presentation to a live audience, encompassing a wide range of settings from small group meetings to large conferences. The confidence required to engage in public speaking effectively is not just about being able to speak clearly and eloquently, but also about mastering the psychological and emotional aspects of communicating with an audience. This confidence can significantly impact a person's ability to convey ideas, persuade others, and lead with authority.

One of the primary elements of confidence in public speaking is thorough preparation. Preparation involves several key steps, starting with understanding the audience. Knowing who the audience is, what their interests and expectations are, and what level of knowledge they have about the topic helps tailor the speech to resonate with them. This understanding can reduce anxiety and boost confidence because the speaker can anticipate the audience's reactions and address their needs effectively.

Researching and organizing content is another critical component of preparation. A well-structured speech with a clear introduction, body, and conclusion provides a roadmap for both the speaker and the audience. When a speaker is confident in their material, it reduces the fear of the unknown and allows for a smoother delivery. Practicing the speech multiple times is essential. Rehearsals help solidify the content, refine delivery, and allow the speaker to become more comfortable with their material. Practicing in front of a mirror, recording oneself, or presenting to a small group of friends or colleagues can provide valuable feedback and increase confidence.

Understanding the importance of body language is also crucial for confident public speaking. Non-verbal communication, such as gestures, eye contact, and posture, significantly influences how a message is received. Confident body language can reinforce the spoken words and convey assurance and authority. Practicing these aspects of delivery helps the speaker feel more in control and project confidence to the audience. For example, maintaining eye contact can make the audience feel engaged and valued, while appropriate gestures can emphasize key points and make the speech more dynamic.

Another significant factor in building confidence for public speaking is the management of anxiety and nervousness. It is natural to feel anxious before speaking in public, but there are strategies to manage this anxiety effectively. Deep breathing exercises, visualization techniques, and positive self-talk can help calm the mind and body. Visualization involves imagining a successful speaking experience, which can create a mental blueprint for success. Positive self-talk involves replacing negative thoughts with affirmations of confidence and competence. These techniques can help reduce anxiety and build a sense of calm and control.

Engaging with the audience is another way to boost confidence. Establishing a connection with the audience through interactive elements, such as asking questions, inviting participation, or sharing personal anecdotes, can make the experience more enjoyable for both the speaker and the audience. This engagement creates a sense of rapport and reduces the feeling of speaking to a faceless crowd. Knowing that the audience is responsive and interested can significantly enhance a speaker's confidence.

Feedback is an invaluable tool for building confidence in public speaking. Constructive feedback from peers, mentors, or audience members provides insights into strengths and areas for improvement. Understanding what worked well and what can be enhanced helps the speaker grow and refine their skills. Over time, incorporating feedback leads to greater confidence as the speaker becomes more proficient and comfortable with public speaking.

Confidence in public speaking also grows with experience. The more opportunities a person has to speak in public, the more familiar and comfortable they become with the process. Each speaking engagement provides a chance to learn, adapt, and improve. Overcoming initial fears and succeeding in public speaking can create a positive feedback loop, where success breeds confidence and confidence breeds further success.

The psychological benefits of confidence in public speaking extend beyond the act of speaking itself. Confident speakers often experience a boost in self-esteem and self-efficacy. They believe in their ability to communicate effectively and influence others, which can translate into other areas of life. This sense of empowerment can enhance personal relationships, career prospects, and overall well-being.

Public speaking also offers numerous professional benefits, making confidence in this area a valuable asset. Effective public speakers can inspire and motivate others, leading to greater leadership opportunities and career advancement. They can articulate their ideas clearly and persuasively, which is crucial in business negotiations, team meetings, and presentations. Confidence in public speaking can set individuals apart in the workplace, demonstrating their competence, leadership potential, and ability to handle challenging situations.

Furthermore, confident public speakers can advocate for important causes and influence public opinion. They have the ability to raise awareness, inspire action, and drive social change. This impact extends to various fields, including politics, education, healthcare, and advocacy work. The ability to speak confidently in public allows individuals to champion their beliefs and make a difference in the world.

The journey to becoming a confident public speaker often involves overcoming personal barriers and fears. Many people experience glossophobia, the fear of public speaking, which can be debilitating. Addressing this fear requires a combination of strategies, including preparation, practice, and mindset shifts. Overcoming glossophobia is a significant achievement that can transform an individual's life, opening up new opportunities and possibilities.

In addition to individual efforts, there are various resources and support systems available to help build confidence in public speaking. Public speaking courses, workshops, and coaching sessions offer structured learning and practice opportunities. Organizations such as Toastmasters International provide a supportive environment for individuals to develop their speaking skills through regular practice and feedback. These resources can be instrumental in building confidence and honing public speaking abilities.

Another critical aspect of confidence in public speaking is the ability to handle unexpected situations and adapt on the fly. Public speaking often involves dealing with unforeseen challenges, such as technical difficulties, difficult questions, or a disengaged audience. A confident speaker can remain composed, think on their feet, and navigate these situations effectively. This adaptability is a hallmark of a skilled public speaker and contributes to their overall confidence.

Storytelling is a powerful tool that can enhance confidence in public speaking. Humans are naturally drawn to stories, and incorporating storytelling elements into a speech can make it more engaging and memorable. Sharing personal stories or using anecdotes to illustrate key points can create an emotional connection with the audience and make the message more relatable. Storytelling also allows the speaker to convey complex ideas in a more accessible and compelling way, boosting their confidence in delivering the message.

Another component of confident public speaking is understanding the importance of pacing and timing. A well-paced speech keeps the audience engaged and ensures that the message is delivered effectively. Practicing pacing, including pauses for emphasis and allowing time for the audience to absorb information, can enhance the overall impact of the speech. Confident speakers are mindful of their timing and can adjust their delivery as needed to maintain audience interest.

The visual aspect of a speech, including the use of visual aids and presentation tools, can also influence confidence. Effective use of visual aids, such as slides, charts, or videos, can enhance the message and provide visual reinforcement of key points. Confident speakers are adept at integrating visual aids seamlessly into their presentation, ensuring that they complement rather than distract from the spoken word. Mastery of these tools adds to the speaker's confidence and enhances the overall effectiveness of the presentation.

Chapter 32: The Comfort of a Well-Organized Home

The comfort of a well-organized home extends far beyond the aesthetic appeal of neat and tidy spaces. It touches upon various aspects of psychological, emotional, and physical well-being, creating an environment that promotes tranquility, productivity, and a sense of control. A well-organized home is not just about having a clutter-free living space; it is about cultivating a lifestyle that prioritizes order, functionality, and harmony. The benefits of an organized home are manifold, influencing daily routines, mental clarity, relationships, and overall quality of life.

The foundation of a well-organized home begins with decluttering. Clutter can be a significant source of stress and anxiety, as it creates a chaotic and overwhelming environment. The process of decluttering involves evaluating possessions and deciding which items are essential and which can be discarded, donated, or stored away. This process, though sometimes challenging, can be incredibly liberating. By removing unnecessary items, individuals create more space and make it easier to maintain order. Decluttering also encourages mindfulness and intentional living, as it requires thoughtful consideration of what truly adds value to one's life.

Once the decluttering process is complete, organizing items in a systematic and logical manner is the next step. This involves creating designated spaces for different categories of items, ensuring that everything has a place. For example, kitchen utensils should be stored together in easily accessible drawers, office supplies should be organized in designated storage solutions, and clothing should be neatly arranged in closets and dressers. This systematic approach reduces the time and effort required to find items, minimizing frustration and enhancing efficiency. When every item has a designated place, it is easier to maintain order and prevent the accumulation of clutter in the future.

A well-organized home also emphasizes the importance of storage solutions. Effective storage solutions are tailored to the specific needs and layout of the home, ensuring that space is utilized optimally. This can include built-in shelves, closet organizers, storage bins, and multi-functional furniture with hidden storage compartments. These solutions help maximize space and keep items neatly tucked away, contributing to a clean and orderly appearance. Additionally, clear labeling of storage containers and shelves can further enhance organization, making it easy to locate and return items to their rightful places.

The physical comfort of a well-organized home is closely linked to its cleanliness and maintenance. Regular cleaning routines are easier to establish and maintain in an organized environment, as there is less clutter to navigate around. A clean home promotes better health by reducing dust, allergens, and germs, creating a safer and more comfortable living space. Routine maintenance tasks, such as repairing broken items or replacing worn-out furnishings, are also more manageable in an organized home. This proactive approach to maintenance helps prevent larger issues from arising and ensures that the home remains in good condition over time.

The psychological benefits of a well-organized home are profound. Living in an orderly environment can significantly reduce stress and anxiety. Clutter and disorganization can contribute to feelings of chaos and overwhelm, whereas a tidy space promotes a sense of calm and control. This sense of order can extend to other areas of life, enhancing overall mental clarity and focus. In an organized home, individuals are better able to concentrate on tasks, make decisions, and manage their time effectively. This can lead to increased productivity and a greater sense of accomplishment.

A well-organized home also fosters emotional well-being by creating a nurturing and supportive environment. The aesthetics of an orderly space, characterized by clean lines, harmonious arrangements, and thoughtfully curated decor, can evoke feelings of peace and satisfaction. Personal touches, such as family photos, cherished mementos, and favorite artwork, can be displayed prominently in an organized home, contributing to a sense of identity and belonging. This emotional connection to one's living space can enhance overall happiness and contentment.

The impact of a well-organized home on relationships should not be underestimated. Shared living spaces, when orderly and well-maintained, can reduce potential sources of conflict and tension among household members. Clear organization and established routines make it easier for everyone to contribute to household tasks and responsibilities, fostering a sense of teamwork and cooperation. Additionally, an organized home can be more inviting for guests, creating a welcoming atmosphere for social interactions and gatherings. This can strengthen relationships and promote a sense of community and connection.

Another significant aspect of the comfort derived from a well-organized home is the sense of preparedness and readiness it imparts. In an organized home, important documents, emergency supplies, and essential items are easily accessible. This preparedness can be crucial in times of need, such as during medical emergencies, natural disasters, or other unforeseen events. Knowing that everything is in its place and readily available can provide peace of mind and reduce the stress associated with emergencies. This level of organization can also extend to financial and administrative aspects of life, with bills, receipts, and important paperwork systematically filed and easily retrievable.

A well-organized home also encourages sustainability and mindful consumption. When items are organized and their quantity and condition are known, it reduces the likelihood of unnecessary purchases and waste. This mindful approach to consumption promotes a more sustainable lifestyle, as individuals are more likely to value and care for their possessions. Additionally, organizing practices such as recycling, composting, and proper disposal of unwanted items contribute to environmental responsibility. An organized home can thus reflect and support a commitment to sustainable living, aligning with broader values of environmental stewardship.

The influence of a well-organized home on personal routines and habits is another important consideration. An orderly environment can facilitate the establishment and maintenance of healthy habits and routines. For example, a well-organized kitchen can make meal planning and preparation more efficient and enjoyable, encouraging healthier eating habits. Similarly, a tidy and organized workspace can enhance focus and productivity, supporting professional and personal goals. By creating an environment that supports and reinforces positive habits, a well-organized home can contribute to overall well-being and success.

In addition to these practical benefits, the comfort of a well-organized home is also deeply tied to its aesthetic appeal. A visually pleasing environment can elevate the mood and create a sense of joy and inspiration. Thoughtful design elements, such as color schemes, lighting, and decor, play a crucial role in enhancing the aesthetic comfort of a home. An organized space allows these design elements to shine, creating a cohesive and harmonious atmosphere. This aesthetic comfort can make daily living more enjoyable and provide a sense of pride and satisfaction in one's home.

The role of technology in achieving and maintaining a well-organized home is increasingly significant. Smart home devices, such as automated lighting, temperature control systems, and security systems, can enhance organization and convenience. Apps and digital tools for task management, home inventory, and scheduling can further streamline household management. By integrating technology into the organization process, individuals can create a more efficient and comfortable living environment. This technological support can also provide valuable assistance for those with busy lifestyles or specific organizational challenges.

The comfort of a well-organized home is ultimately a reflection of the values and priorities of its inhabitants. It embodies a commitment to order, functionality, and beauty, creating a space that supports physical health, mental clarity, emotional well-being, and harmonious relationships. The process of organizing and maintaining a home is an ongoing journey that requires attention, effort, and intention. However, the rewards of this effort are immense, offering a sanctuary of comfort and peace in an often chaotic world. By prioritizing organization, individuals can transform their living spaces into havens of tranquility and efficiency, enhancing their quality of life and fostering a greater sense of satisfaction and fulfillment.

Chapter 33: Discovering New Hobbies

Discovering new hobbies is a journey of self-exploration, creativity, and enrichment that can profoundly impact one's quality of life. Hobbies are activities undertaken for pleasure and relaxation during one's leisure time, and they offer numerous benefits, including stress relief, personal growth, and the development of new skills. Engaging in a variety of hobbies can lead to a more fulfilling and balanced life, providing opportunities to discover new interests, connect with others, and cultivate a sense of achievement and joy. The process of discovering new hobbies involves exploring different activities, trying new things, and finding what resonates personally.

The first step in discovering new hobbies is to assess one's interests and curiosities. This involves reflecting on what activities bring joy, satisfaction, or intrigue. Sometimes, it's about reconnecting with interests from childhood or adolescence that may have been set aside due to life's demands. For instance, a person who loved drawing or painting as a child might find great fulfillment in rediscovering that passion as an adult. Similarly, someone who enjoyed playing sports or being outdoors may find new hobbies in activities like hiking, cycling, or team sports. Revisiting these interests can spark inspiration and lead to the exploration of new and related hobbies.

Another important aspect of discovering new hobbies is being open to experimentation. This means stepping out of one's comfort zone and trying activities that may not initially seem appealing or familiar. Experimentation can be both exciting and challenging, as it requires a willingness to embrace new experiences and possibly confront fears or insecurities. This process of trial and error is crucial because it allows individuals to explore a wide range of activities and identify what truly captivates them. For example, attending a pottery class, taking up gardening, or joining a book club are all ways to experiment with new hobbies. Each experience provides valuable insights into personal preferences and interests.

The social aspect of discovering new hobbies is also significant. Many hobbies provide opportunities to meet new people and build connections. Joining clubs, groups, or classes related to specific interests can create a sense of community and belonging. These social interactions not only make the experience of learning a new hobby more enjoyable but also provide motivation and support. For instance, participating in a dance class, a cooking workshop, or a photography club allows individuals to share their passion with like-minded people, exchange ideas, and develop friendships. The camaraderie and encouragement from others can enhance the overall experience and make the pursuit of a new hobby more rewarding.

Exploring hobbies that involve learning new skills can be particularly gratifying. Hobbies such as playing a musical instrument, learning a new language, or mastering a craft like woodworking or knitting require dedication and practice. The process of acquiring and honing new skills can boost self-confidence and provide a sense of accomplishment. These hobbies often have a steep learning curve, but the progress made over time can be immensely satisfying. The skills gained through these hobbies can also be practical and useful in everyday life, adding to their value and appeal.

Travel and cultural exploration can be a rich source of inspiration for discovering new hobbies. Exposure to different cultures, traditions, and ways of life can introduce individuals to unique activities and interests they may not have encountered otherwise. For example, traveling to a country known for its culinary traditions might inspire someone to take up cooking or baking as a hobby. Similarly, visiting a region with a rich history of craftsmanship might spark an interest in pottery, weaving, or other traditional arts. Cultural festivals, markets, and workshops can provide hands-on experiences and deepen one's appreciation for these activities.

Technology and the digital age have opened up a plethora of opportunities for discovering new hobbies. The internet is a vast resource for finding information, tutorials, and communities related to almost any interest imaginable. Online platforms such as YouTube, Udemy, and Skillshare offer courses and instructional videos on a wide range of hobbies, from coding and graphic design to yoga and meditation. Social media platforms and online forums also provide spaces for individuals to share their experiences, seek advice, and connect with others who share similar interests. This accessibility makes it easier than ever to explore new hobbies from the comfort of one's home.

Reading and literature can also play a pivotal role in discovering new hobbies. Books, magazines, and blogs offer a wealth of knowledge and inspiration on various topics. Reading about different hobbies, the experiences of others, and the benefits associated with them can ignite curiosity and motivation to try something new. For example, reading a memoir by an avid gardener might inspire someone to start their own garden, or a book about the adventures of a mountain climber might spark an interest in hiking and outdoor exploration. Literature provides not only information but also a narrative that can make hobbies come to life in a vivid and compelling way.

The process of discovering new hobbies often involves a degree of self-discovery and personal growth. Engaging in new activities can reveal hidden talents and passions, providing deeper insights into one's preferences and capabilities. This self-discovery can lead to increased self-awareness and a better understanding of what brings joy and fulfillment. Additionally, the challenges and successes encountered while pursuing new hobbies can build resilience and confidence, fostering a growth mindset. Embracing new hobbies as a form of self-expression and creativity can also enhance overall well-being and mental health.

Balancing multiple hobbies can be a rewarding way to diversify interests and prevent burnout. Having a variety of hobbies allows individuals to switch between different activities based on their mood, energy levels, and available time. For instance, someone might enjoy the physical activity of running or playing sports while also appreciating the quiet and meditative aspects of painting or reading. This balance can keep the experience of engaging in hobbies fresh and exciting, preventing monotony and maintaining enthusiasm. It also provides a holistic approach to personal enrichment, addressing different aspects of mental, physical, and emotional well-being.

For those who are unsure where to start in discovering new hobbies, seeking recommendations and inspiration from others can be helpful. Friends, family members, colleagues, and mentors can offer valuable suggestions based on their own experiences and interests. Attending local events, visiting hobby stores, and exploring community centers can also provide ideas and opportunities to try new activities. Sometimes, a simple conversation or a casual visit to a new place can spark an interest that leads to the discovery of a new hobby.

The benefits of discovering new hobbies extend beyond personal enjoyment and fulfillment. Hobbies can also provide a sense of purpose and direction, particularly during times of transition or uncertainty. For example, retirement, career changes, or significant life events can leave individuals searching for new ways to spend their time and energy. Engaging in hobbies can provide a constructive and meaningful outlet, offering a sense of continuity and stability. Hobbies can also serve as a form of escapism, providing a temporary respite from the stresses and pressures of daily life.

Financial considerations are an important aspect of discovering new hobbies. While some hobbies may require an initial investment in equipment, materials, or classes, many can be pursued on a budget or even for free. For instance, hiking, reading, writing, and drawing can be relatively low-cost hobbies. Public libraries, community centers, and online resources often provide access to materials and opportunities to learn new skills without significant expense. Being mindful of the financial aspect ensures that hobbies remain a source of joy and relaxation rather than stress or burden.

The longevity and evolution of hobbies are also worth considering. Some hobbies may remain a lifelong passion, while others might evolve or change over time. It is natural for interests to shift as individuals grow and their circumstances change. The flexibility to adapt and explore new hobbies ensures that the pursuit of personal interests remains dynamic and engaging. Revisiting old hobbies with a new perspective or combining different interests to create unique hybrid hobbies can also be a source of innovation and excitement.

Chapter 34: The Fulfillment of Volunteer Work

The fulfillment of volunteer work is a profound and multifaceted experience that impacts not only the individuals who engage in it but also the communities and causes they support. Volunteer work is the act of offering one's time, skills, and energy without monetary compensation to help others or advance a cause. This altruistic activity can take many forms, from local community service and international aid to environmental conservation and advocacy efforts. The sense of fulfillment derived from volunteer work arises from a combination of personal growth, social connections, and the tangible positive impact made on the lives of others.

One of the primary sources of fulfillment in volunteer work is the sense of purpose it provides. Many individuals seek out volunteer opportunities to give their lives greater meaning and to contribute to something larger than themselves. This sense of purpose can be incredibly motivating and can drive individuals to dedicate significant time and effort to their chosen cause. Knowing that one's actions are making a difference, whether it is feeding the homeless, tutoring disadvantaged children, or participating in environmental clean-ups, instills a deep sense of satisfaction and fulfillment. This purpose-driven engagement often translates into a greater overall sense of well-being and life satisfaction.

Personal growth and development are significant benefits of volunteer work. Engaging in volunteer activities allows individuals to develop new skills, gain valuable experience, and broaden their perspectives. For example, volunteering at a healthcare facility can provide insights into medical professions and patient care, while working with a non-profit organization can enhance skills in project management, fundraising, and communication. These experiences not only enhance one's resume but also contribute to personal enrichment and self-improvement. The challenges encountered during volunteer work, such as problem-solving in resource-limited settings or managing diverse groups of people, build resilience and adaptability, which are valuable life skills.

Social connections and the sense of community fostered through volunteer work are also key components of its fulfillment. Volunteering often brings together individuals from various backgrounds who share a common goal or passion. These interactions can lead to the formation of meaningful relationships and friendships. The camaraderie and mutual support experienced among volunteers create a sense of belonging and connectedness. Volunteering can also strengthen ties within a community, as individuals come together to address local issues and support each other. This sense of community can be particularly important for those who may feel isolated or disconnected, providing a network of support and shared purpose.

The emotional and psychological benefits of volunteer work are well-documented. Numerous studies have shown that volunteering is associated with lower levels of depression, anxiety, and stress. Engaging in altruistic activities can boost mood and increase feelings of happiness and contentment. This "helper's high" is attributed to the release of endorphins and other positive neurotransmitters in the brain. Additionally, volunteering can provide a sense of accomplishment and pride, as individuals see the direct results of their efforts and contributions. This positive feedback loop reinforces the desire to continue volunteering and contributes to overall mental health and well-being.

The fulfillment of volunteer work is also closely tied to the impact it has on the beneficiaries. Seeing the positive changes and improvements resulting from one's efforts can be incredibly rewarding. For example, volunteers who participate in literacy programs may witness the progress of students as they develop reading and writing skills. Those involved in building homes for the underprivileged can see families move into safe and secure housing. Environmental volunteers might observe the restoration of natural habitats and the return of wildlife. These tangible outcomes provide a clear and direct sense of accomplishment and reinforce the value of volunteer work.

Volunteering can also enhance one's understanding and empathy for others. Working with diverse populations and witnessing the challenges faced by different communities can broaden perspectives and foster a deeper appreciation for the complexities of social issues. This increased empathy can lead to greater tolerance, compassion, and a commitment to social justice. Volunteers often report a heightened awareness of societal needs and a desire to advocate for positive change. This advocacy can extend beyond volunteer activities, influencing personal and professional choices and promoting a more compassionate and equitable society.

The flexibility and variety of volunteer opportunities contribute to their appeal and fulfillment. Volunteer work can be tailored to fit individual interests, skills, and schedules. From short-term projects to long-term commitments, there are opportunities to suit everyone's availability and preferences. This flexibility allows individuals to engage in volunteer work that aligns with their passions and expertise, making the experience more enjoyable and meaningful. For example, someone with a background in education might find fulfillment in tutoring or mentoring, while a person with a passion for the environment might enjoy participating in conservation efforts. The ability to choose volunteer activities that resonate personally enhances the overall sense of fulfillment.

Volunteering can also serve as a bridge to new opportunities and career paths. For many, volunteer work provides valuable experience and networking opportunities that can lead to paid employment or career advancement. It offers a way to explore different fields and industries, gain practical skills, and demonstrate commitment and initiative to potential employers. In some cases, volunteer work can even lead to job offers within the organization or sector one is passionate about. This potential for professional growth adds an additional layer of fulfillment, as individuals can see their volunteer efforts translate into career success and advancement.

The intergenerational aspect of volunteer work is another source of fulfillment. Volunteering provides opportunities for people of all ages to work together toward common goals, fostering mutual respect and understanding between generations. Younger volunteers can learn from the experience and wisdom of older volunteers, while older volunteers can gain fresh perspectives and energy from younger participants. This intergenerational collaboration enriches the volunteer experience and strengthens community bonds. It also provides a platform for passing down values of service, compassion, and civic responsibility to future generations.

The global perspective gained through international volunteer work can be particularly transformative. Volunteering abroad exposes individuals to different cultures, languages, and ways of life, fostering cross-cultural understanding and global citizenship. These experiences can be eye-opening and humbling, highlighting both the similarities and differences between people worldwide. International volunteers often develop a deeper appreciation for diversity and a commitment to addressing global issues such as poverty, healthcare, and education. The fulfillment derived from making a positive impact on a global scale can be immense, reinforcing the interconnectedness of humanity and the importance of global solidarity.

Volunteer work also offers a sense of continuity and stability, particularly during times of personal or societal upheaval. In moments of crisis, such as natural disasters, pandemics, or economic downturns, volunteering provides a constructive way to channel energy and resources into helping others. This proactive engagement can mitigate feelings of helplessness and provide a sense of control and purpose.

Volunteering during challenging times can also foster resilience and a collective spirit of recovery and rebuilding. Knowing that one is contributing to the greater good and supporting those in need can be a powerful source of fulfillment and hope.

For retirees or those with more free time, volunteering can offer a meaningful way to stay active and engaged. Transitioning from a busy career to retirement can sometimes lead to feelings of boredom or loss of identity. Volunteering provides a purposeful way to fill time and continue contributing to society. It offers structure and routine, opportunities for social interaction, and a sense of achievement. Many retirees find great fulfillment in using their skills and experience to give back to the community, whether through mentoring, consulting, or direct service. This continued engagement in meaningful activities can enhance overall well-being and life satisfaction in later years.

The fulfillment of volunteer work is not limited to the individual level; it also extends to the broader community and society. Volunteers play a crucial role in addressing social issues, supporting vulnerable populations, and enhancing the quality of life in their communities. Their contributions can fill gaps in services, provide vital support to non-profit organizations, and drive positive social change. The collective impact of volunteer efforts can lead to stronger, more resilient communities and a more just and equitable society. This broader perspective on the significance of volunteer work can deepen the sense of fulfillment for those who participate, knowing that they are part of a larger movement for good.

Chapter 35: Learning a New Language

Learning a new language is an enriching and multifaceted endeavor that can have profound impacts on an individual's cognitive abilities, cultural understanding, social connections, and career opportunities. The process of acquiring a new language involves mastering vocabulary, grammar, pronunciation, and the ability to comprehend and produce both spoken and written forms of the language. This undertaking requires dedication, practice, and often, immersion in environments where the language is used. The journey of learning a new language is not only about acquiring a new skill but also about opening doors to new experiences and perspectives.

One of the most significant cognitive benefits of learning a new language is the enhancement of brain function. Numerous studies have shown that bilingualism and multilingualism improve cognitive abilities, such as problem-solving, multitasking, and decision-making. Learning a new language exercises the brain by challenging it to recognize, negotiate meaning, and communicate in different linguistic systems. This mental workout can enhance overall cognitive flexibility, which is the brain's ability to switch between different tasks or thoughts seamlessly. Additionally, bilingual individuals often show improved memory and are better at tasks that require creative thinking. The cognitive benefits of language learning can also contribute to delaying the onset of age-related cognitive decline, such as dementia and Alzheimer's disease.

Another profound impact of learning a new language is the cultural awareness and appreciation it fosters. Language and culture are deeply intertwined, and learning a new language provides insights into the customs, traditions, and worldviews of the people who speak it. This cultural immersion can lead to greater empathy, tolerance, and understanding of different ways of life. For example, learning Japanese might introduce a student to the concepts of respect and hierarchy that are deeply embedded in Japanese society, while learning Spanish could provide a window into the diverse cultures of Latin America. This cultural competence is increasingly valuable in our globalized world, where cross-cultural communication and collaboration are essential.

Social connections and opportunities for building relationships are another significant benefit of learning a new language. Being able to communicate in another language opens up new social circles and allows for more meaningful interactions with people from different linguistic backgrounds. This can lead to friendships, professional networks, and even romantic relationships that would not have been possible otherwise. For instance, someone learning French might connect with French-speaking communities locally or internationally, participate in cultural exchange programs, or travel more confidently to French-speaking countries. These social interactions enrich personal life and broaden one's social horizons.

Learning a new language can also significantly enhance career prospects and professional development. In many industries, bilingualism or multilingualism is a highly sought-after skill. Employers often value employees who can communicate with international clients, partners, and colleagues, as this ability can facilitate business operations and expand market reach. Language skills can lead to job opportunities in fields such as translation, interpretation, international relations, tourism, and global business. Furthermore, language proficiency can differentiate job candidates in competitive fields, making them more attractive to potential employers. For example, proficiency in Mandarin Chinese, given China's significant role in the global economy, can be a considerable asset in international business and trade.

The personal satisfaction and confidence that come from learning a new language are also noteworthy. Mastering a language, even at a basic level, is a significant achievement that requires dedication and effort. This accomplishment can boost self-esteem and provide a sense of pride. The ability to understand and be understood in another language is empowering and can enhance travel experiences, allowing for deeper connections with local people and cultures. Moreover, the process of learning a new language often involves overcoming challenges and stepping out of one's comfort zone, which can foster resilience and a growth mindset. These personal qualities are valuable not only in language learning but in all areas of life.

Language learning also promotes better listening and communication skills. The process of acquiring a new language requires careful listening to understand pronunciation, intonation, and nuances. This heightened awareness of sound patterns can improve one's ability to listen and communicate effectively, even in their native language. Effective communication is not just about speaking but also about understanding and responding appropriately to others. The patience and attention to detail developed through language learning can enhance interpersonal communication skills, making individuals better listeners and more thoughtful communicators.

The practical benefits of learning a new language extend to travel and exploration. Knowing the local language can significantly enhance travel experiences by making it easier to navigate, interact with locals, and access services. Travelers who speak the local language can immerse themselves more fully in the culture, participate in local customs, and explore off-the-beaten-path destinations that might be inaccessible without language skills. This deeper engagement with the local environment leads to more authentic and memorable travel experiences. Additionally, language skills can provide a sense of security and independence when traveling, as travelers can handle emergencies, seek assistance, and understand important information more effectively.

Learning a new language also offers numerous health benefits. The mental exercise involved in language learning stimulates the brain and promotes neuroplasticity, which is the brain's ability to reorganize itself by forming new neural connections. This ongoing mental activity can help maintain brain health and cognitive function throughout life. Studies have shown that bilingual individuals tend to have better mental health outcomes and lower rates of depression and anxiety. Engaging in language learning can also provide a sense of purpose and structure, which can contribute to overall well-being and life satisfaction.

The process of learning a new language can be greatly enhanced by various tools and resources available today. Technology has revolutionized language learning, making it more accessible and interactive. Online courses, language learning apps, and virtual language exchange platforms provide flexible and convenient ways to practice and improve language skills. These resources often incorporate multimedia elements, such as videos, audio recordings, and interactive exercises, which cater to different learning styles and keep learners engaged. Additionally, many language learning platforms offer opportunities to connect with native speakers for practice and cultural exchange, further enriching the learning experience.

Immersive experiences, such as studying abroad, participating in language immersion programs, or living in a country where the language is spoken, are highly effective ways to accelerate language learning. Immersion forces learners to use the language in real-life situations, enhancing their proficiency and fluency. This type of experiential learning goes beyond classroom instruction and textbooks, providing practical, hands-on opportunities to practice speaking, listening, reading, and writing. The cultural exposure gained through immersion also deepens understanding and appreciation of the language, making the learning process more holistic and impactful.

Another important aspect of language learning is the development of intercultural communication skills. Effective communication in a new language involves understanding not just the words but also the cultural context in which they are used. This includes non-verbal communication, such as gestures, body language, and social norms. For example, in some cultures, maintaining eye contact is a sign of confidence and honesty, while in others, it might be considered rude or confrontational. Learning these subtleties is crucial for effective and respectful communication. Intercultural communication skills are valuable in both personal and professional settings, fostering better relationships and collaboration in diverse environments.

The discipline and persistence required to learn a new language can translate into other areas of life. Language learning is a long-term commitment that involves regular practice, setting goals, and tracking progress. This disciplined approach can enhance time management skills and self-discipline, which are beneficial for achieving other personal and professional goals. The experience of working towards language proficiency can also build resilience and a positive attitude towards learning and growth. Overcoming the challenges of language learning can instill a sense of perseverance and determination that can be applied to various pursuits.

In educational settings, language learning can enrich the academic experience and enhance students' overall education. Bilingual education programs, where subjects are taught in two languages, can improve cognitive development and academic performance. Learning a new language can also enhance understanding of other academic subjects, such as history, literature, and social studies, by providing a broader cultural context. For example, studying Spanish literature can offer insights into the historical and cultural developments of Spanish-speaking countries. This interdisciplinary approach enriches the educational experience and fosters a more comprehensive understanding of the world.

For children, learning a new language at an early age can be particularly beneficial. Young children have a natural ability to acquire languages more easily than adults, and being bilingual or multilingual from a young age can enhance cognitive development and academic performance. Early language learning can also promote cultural awareness and sensitivity, helping children develop an appreciation for diversity and inclusivity. Additionally, children who grow up bilingual or multilingual often have better language skills overall, including in their native language, and are more adept at learning additional languages in the future.

Community and societal benefits also arise from widespread language learning. In multicultural societies, language skills can promote social cohesion and mutual understanding among diverse groups. Bilingualism and multilingualism can bridge communication gaps, reduce cultural barriers, and foster a sense of community. For example, in countries with large immigrant populations, language programs can help newcomers integrate more effectively, access services, and participate fully in society. Language learning initiatives can also preserve linguistic diversity and promote the revitalization of endangered languages, contributing to the preservation of cultural heritage.

Chapter 36: The Thrill of Planning a Future Trip

The thrill of planning a future trip is an exhilarating and multi-layered experience that involves anticipation, research, and imagination. This process starts the moment one decides to embark on a new adventure, igniting a sense of excitement and curiosity about the unknown. The anticipation of exploring new destinations, cultures, and experiences fuels the planning process, making it a journey in itself.

Initially, the idea of a future trip sparks a sense of wanderlust. The mere thought of escaping daily routines and venturing into uncharted territories creates a feeling of freedom and possibility. Whether it's a solo journey, a romantic getaway, a family vacation, or a trip with friends, the excitement begins as soon as the decision is made. This initial stage is often filled with daydreams and what-if scenarios, imagining the places to be visited, the people to be met, and the experiences to be had.

Researching destinations is a crucial part of the planning process and adds to the excitement. Exploring potential destinations involves reading travel blogs, watching videos, and scrolling through social media feeds filled with stunning images. This research phase can be incredibly engaging, as it allows travelers to discover hidden gems, iconic landmarks, and unique experiences. From browsing guidebooks to following travel influencers, gathering information helps shape the vision of the trip. This stage is also where one begins to learn about the culture, history, and traditions of the chosen destination, deepening the connection to the upcoming adventure.

Creating an itinerary is another thrilling aspect of trip planning. Mapping out the journey day by day involves deciding on key attractions, activities, and experiences. This process requires careful consideration of what each destination has to offer and how to make the most of the time available. Whether it's visiting world-famous landmarks, hiking in national parks, indulging in local cuisine, or exploring off-the-beaten-path locations, crafting an itinerary is like piecing together a puzzle. Each decision brings the trip closer to reality, and the anticipation builds with each new addition to the plan.

Booking accommodations and transportation further solidifies the trip's reality. Choosing where to stay, from luxury hotels to cozy bed and breakfasts or unique vacation rentals, adds a layer of excitement. Each option offers a different experience, whether it's waking up to a view of the ocean, staying in a historic city center, or enjoying the tranquility of a rural retreat. Similarly, booking flights, trains, or car rentals involves logistical planning that brings the dream closer to fruition. The confirmation emails and booking references serve as tangible proof that the adventure is real and approaching.

Planning activities and experiences is a particularly thrilling part of preparing for a trip. This involves researching and selecting tours, excursions, and events that align with personal interests and passions. For some, it might be exploring ancient ruins and historical sites; for others, it could be adrenaline-pumping activities like zip-lining, scuba diving, or skiing. Food enthusiasts might plan their trip around culinary experiences, seeking out the best local restaurants, street food vendors, and cooking classes. Each planned activity adds to the anticipation and helps create a vivid picture of the trip ahead.

Learning basic phrases in the local language can also enhance the excitement of planning a trip. Familiarizing oneself with common greetings, expressions, and useful phrases not only helps with practical communication but also deepens the connection to the destination. This linguistic preparation can be both fun and educational, providing a sense of accomplishment and readiness. Engaging with the language of the destination fosters a sense of respect and appreciation for the culture and can lead to more meaningful interactions during the trip.

Shopping for the trip is another delightful aspect of the planning process. Gathering travel essentials, such as clothing, accessories, and gear, contributes to the anticipation. Whether it's purchasing a new suitcase, comfortable walking shoes, or a travel guidebook, each item adds to the excitement. Packing lists and shopping sprees become part of the ritual, ensuring that everything needed for the adventure is ready and organized. This stage often includes imagining oneself in different scenarios, from lounging on a beach to exploring bustling markets, further fueling the excitement.

Financial planning and budgeting are essential components of trip preparation. Allocating funds for different aspects of the trip, such as transportation, accommodation, food, and activities, ensures that the adventure is both enjoyable and financially manageable. This process involves comparing prices, seeking out deals, and sometimes making trade-offs to stay within budget. While it may seem practical, financial planning also adds to the thrill, as it involves making choices that shape the overall experience. Successfully managing the budget provides a sense of accomplishment and peace of mind, knowing that the trip is well-planned and financially feasible.

Sharing the trip plans with friends and family adds another layer of excitement. Discussing the itinerary, sharing travel tips, and seeking advice from those who have visited the destination before creates a sense of community and shared anticipation. This social aspect of trip planning can lead to valuable insights and recommendations, making the trip even more enriching. Additionally, sharing the excitement with others often results in supportive and enthusiastic responses, further amplifying the anticipation.

For those who enjoy photography or videography, planning a future trip involves envisioning the moments to capture. Imagining the scenic landscapes, vibrant street scenes, and candid moments creates a sense of purpose and creativity. Planning the types of shots and the equipment needed can be a thrilling part of the preparation, as it combines the excitement of travel with the passion for visual storytelling. The anticipation of capturing and sharing the trip's experiences through photos and videos adds an artistic dimension to the journey.

Anticipation is a powerful emotion that can enhance the overall experience of a trip. Studies have shown that the act of anticipating a pleasurable event can be as enjoyable as the event itself. The weeks or months leading up to the trip are filled with positive emotions and excitement, contributing to overall happiness and well-being. This period of anticipation allows travelers to mentally prepare for the adventure, creating a sense of mindfulness and presence. The thrill of looking forward to new experiences can uplift the spirit and provide a sense of joy and purpose.

Visualizing the trip and setting intentions are integral parts of the planning process. Imagining oneself in different scenarios, from exploring historic sites to relaxing on a beach, creates vivid mental images that bring the trip to life. This visualization can also include setting personal goals or intentions for the trip, such as seeking relaxation, adventure, cultural immersion, or personal growth. These intentions help shape the experience and provide a sense of direction and purpose. The act of visualizing and setting intentions enhances the emotional connection to the trip and deepens the sense of anticipation.

Planning for contingencies and unexpected events is an important aspect of trip preparation. Considering potential challenges and creating backup plans ensures that the trip can proceed smoothly despite unforeseen circumstances. This might involve researching travel insurance, understanding local emergency services, or preparing for weather variations. While it may seem pragmatic, this planning adds to the thrill by creating a sense of readiness and confidence. Knowing that one is prepared for any eventuality provides peace of mind and allows for a more relaxed and enjoyable trip.

The final countdown to the trip is perhaps the most exhilarating phase of the planning process. As the departure date approaches, the excitement reaches its peak. Last-minute preparations, such as packing, confirming reservations, and organizing travel documents, create a flurry of activity. This period is often filled with a mix of emotions, including excitement, nervousness, and anticipation. The realization that the long-awaited adventure is just around the corner brings a sense of urgency and immediacy. Each day brings the traveler closer to the experience, heightening the sense of thrill.

On the eve of the trip, the excitement becomes almost palpable. The suitcase is packed, the itinerary is set, and the traveler is ready to embark on the adventure. This final stage of anticipation is filled with a sense of accomplishment and readiness. The mind is filled with thoughts of the journey ahead, and sleep might be elusive due to the excitement. The anticipation of waking up the next day and starting the trip creates a unique blend of emotions that can only be described as thrilling.

Chapter 37: Overcoming Procrastination

Overcoming procrastination is a complex yet achievable endeavor that requires understanding its root causes, implementing effective strategies, and maintaining consistent effort. Procrastination, the act of delaying or postponing tasks, can significantly hinder personal and professional growth. It often leads to stress, missed opportunities, and feelings of guilt and inadequacy. However, with the right approaches, overcoming procrastination can lead to increased productivity, improved well-being, and a greater sense of accomplishment.

The first step in overcoming procrastination is understanding its underlying causes. Procrastination is not merely a time management issue; it is often rooted in deeper psychological factors. Fear of failure, perfectionism, and lack of motivation are common contributors. Fear of failure can paralyze individuals, making them avoid tasks to evade potential negative outcomes. Perfectionism creates an unrealistic standard, causing individuals to delay tasks until they believe they can perform them flawlessly. Lack of motivation, often stemming from unclear goals or lack of interest, can also lead to procrastination. Identifying these root causes is crucial for developing effective strategies to combat procrastination.

One effective strategy for overcoming procrastination is setting clear, achievable goals. Vague or overwhelming tasks can be daunting and lead to procrastination. Breaking down tasks into smaller, manageable steps can make them less intimidating and more approachable. Setting specific, measurable, attainable, relevant, and time-bound (SMART) goals can provide a clear roadmap and make progress tangible. For example, instead of setting a goal to "write a report," a more specific goal would be "write the introduction of the report by the end of the day." This approach not only clarifies what needs to be done but also creates a sense of urgency and direction.

Time management techniques are essential tools in the battle against procrastination. One such technique is the Pomodoro Technique, which involves working for a set period (usually 25 minutes) followed by a short break. This method helps maintain focus and prevent burnout by breaking work into manageable intervals. Another useful technique is time blocking, which involves scheduling specific blocks of time for different tasks. By allocating dedicated time slots for each task, individuals can create a structured and organized approach to their work. Prioritizing tasks using methods such as the Eisenhower Matrix, which categorizes tasks based on their urgency and importance, can also help individuals focus on what truly matters and avoid getting sidetracked by less critical activities.

Developing self-discipline and building healthy habits are crucial components of overcoming procrastination. Self-discipline involves the ability to stay focused and committed to tasks despite distractions and temptations. Building healthy habits, such as starting the day with a specific routine or setting aside regular time for work, can create a sense of structure and consistency. Implementing habits such as regular exercise, adequate sleep, and a balanced diet can also enhance overall well-being and productivity. Self-discipline can be strengthened through practices such as mindfulness and meditation, which improve focus and self-awareness. By cultivating these habits, individuals can create an environment that supports productivity and reduces the likelihood of procrastination.

Creating a conducive work environment is another important factor in overcoming procrastination. A cluttered or distracting workspace can make it difficult to focus and increase the tendency to procrastinate. Organizing the workspace, eliminating distractions, and creating a comfortable and inspiring environment can enhance productivity. This might involve decluttering the desk, ensuring proper lighting, and minimizing noise. For some, background music or white noise can help maintain focus. Additionally, establishing boundaries between work and leisure spaces can help create a mental separation that reinforces the distinction between work time and relaxation time.

Understanding and managing emotions play a significant role in overcoming procrastination. Procrastination is often a coping mechanism for dealing with negative emotions such as anxiety, frustration, or boredom. Developing emotional intelligence, which involves recognizing and understanding one's emotions and their impact on behavior, can help address the emotional aspects of procrastination. Techniques such as cognitive-behavioral therapy (CBT) can be effective in identifying and challenging negative thought patterns that contribute to procrastination. For example, reframing thoughts from "I can't do this perfectly, so I won't do it at all" to "I can do this to the best of my ability, and that's enough" can reduce the pressure and make it easier to start tasks.

Accountability and support systems can be powerful motivators in overcoming procrastination. Sharing goals and progress with friends, family, or colleagues can create a sense of responsibility and encouragement. Accountability partners can provide support, motivation, and constructive feedback, making it more difficult to procrastinate. Joining study groups, productivity communities, or online forums can also offer a sense of camaraderie and shared purpose. In professional settings, regular check-ins with supervisors or team members can help maintain focus and ensure progress. Knowing that someone else is aware of one's commitments and progress can provide an extra push to stay on track.

Reward systems and positive reinforcement can also be effective in combating procrastination. Setting up a system of rewards for completing tasks or reaching milestones can create positive incentives and make the process more enjoyable. Rewards can be small, such as taking a short break, enjoying a favorite snack, or engaging in a preferred activity. Positive reinforcement can boost motivation and create a sense of achievement, making it easier to tackle subsequent tasks. Celebrating small victories and acknowledging progress can build momentum and confidence, reinforcing productive behavior and reducing the tendency to procrastinate.

Mindfulness and self-compassion are important practices in addressing procrastination. Mindfulness involves staying present and fully engaging with the current task, which can reduce distractions and increase focus. Mindfulness practices such as meditation, deep breathing, and mindful movement can enhance concentration and reduce stress. Self-compassion involves treating oneself with kindness and understanding, especially in the face of setbacks or challenges. Recognizing that procrastination is a common human experience and forgiving oneself for past procrastination can reduce self-criticism and create a more positive and supportive mindset. By practicing mindfulness and self-compassion, individuals can develop a healthier relationship with their work and reduce the negative emotions that contribute to procrastination.

Identifying and addressing procrastination triggers is crucial for developing effective strategies. Procrastination triggers can vary from person to person and may include specific tasks, environments, or emotional states. Keeping a procrastination journal can help identify patterns and triggers. By recording when and why procrastination occurs, individuals can gain insights into the underlying causes and develop targeted strategies to address them. For example, if procrastination tends to occur during certain times of the day, adjusting the schedule to tackle challenging tasks during peak productivity hours can be helpful. If specific tasks are particularly daunting, breaking them down into smaller steps or seeking additional support can make them more manageable.

Overcoming procrastination also involves developing a growth mindset. A growth mindset, as opposed to a fixed mindset, involves believing that abilities and skills can be developed through effort and learning. Embracing a growth mindset can reduce the fear of failure and increase resilience in the face of challenges. Viewing tasks as opportunities for growth and learning, rather than as tests of inherent ability, can create a more positive and proactive approach to work. Celebrating effort and progress, rather than focusing solely on outcomes, can reinforce a growth-oriented perspective and reduce the tendency to procrastinate.

Seeking professional help can be beneficial for individuals who struggle with chronic procrastination. Procrastination can be a symptom of underlying issues such as anxiety, depression, attention deficit hyperactivity disorder (ADHD), or other mental health conditions. Consulting with a therapist, counselor, or coach can provide additional support and strategies tailored to individual needs. Therapy can help address the emotional and psychological aspects of procrastination, while coaching can provide practical tools and accountability. Professional help can offer a comprehensive approach to overcoming procrastination and improving overall well-being and productivity.

Chapter 38: The Satisfaction of Helping a Neighbor

The satisfaction of helping a neighbor is a profound and multifaceted experience that touches on aspects of human nature, community, empathy, and personal fulfillment. This satisfaction stems from the innate human desire to connect with others and contribute to the well-being of those around us. Helping a neighbor can take many forms, ranging from simple acts of kindness, such as lending a hand with groceries, to more significant gestures like assisting in times of crisis or offering emotional support. The joy and contentment derived from these actions are deeply rooted in our social instincts and the recognition of our shared humanity. Moreover, helping a neighbor often leads to a sense of community, fosters stronger relationships, and contributes to a more compassionate and supportive environment.

One of the fundamental aspects of the satisfaction derived from helping a neighbor is the feeling of connection it fosters. Humans are inherently social beings, and our well-being is closely tied to our relationships and interactions with others. When we help a neighbor, we engage in a reciprocal relationship that goes beyond the act itself. This connection is built on empathy, understanding, and the recognition of shared experiences and challenges. For example, helping a neighbor with their garden or shoveling snow from their driveway is not just about the task at hand; it is also about the conversation, the shared smiles, and the sense of camaraderie that develops. This connection can be particularly meaningful in a world where people often feel isolated or disconnected from their communities.

Another important aspect of helping a neighbor is the cultivation of empathy and compassion. When we take the time to help others, we often gain a deeper understanding of their circumstances and challenges. This perspective can foster a greater sense of empathy, as we recognize that everyone has struggles and that a small act of kindness can make a significant difference in someone's day. For instance, offering to babysit for a single parent or providing a meal for a neighbor who is recovering from surgery can ease their burdens and provide comfort during a difficult time. These acts of kindness are not just beneficial for the recipients; they also enrich the giver's life by broadening their perspective and deepening their capacity for compassion.

The satisfaction of helping a neighbor is also closely tied to the sense of purpose and fulfillment it provides. Many people find that acts of kindness and service give their lives meaning and direction. This is often because these actions align with deeply held values, such as generosity, compassion, and community. Helping others can be a way of living out these values in practical and tangible ways. For example, a person who values environmental sustainability might help a neighbor set up a composting system or organize a community recycling program. These actions not only contribute to the well-being of the community but also provide the individual with a sense of purpose and alignment with their values.

Additionally, helping a neighbor can lead to the development of new skills and experiences. Engaging in acts of service often requires problem-solving, creativity, and collaboration. For instance, organizing a neighborhood clean-up or planning a community event can involve logistical planning, communication, and coordination with others. These activities can be personally enriching, providing opportunities to learn new skills, build confidence, and expand one's horizons. They can also foster a sense of accomplishment and pride, as individuals see the tangible impact of their efforts. This personal growth and development are often accompanied by a sense of joy and satisfaction, as helping others brings about positive change and strengthens the community.

The act of helping a neighbor also contributes to the creation of a supportive and resilient community. Communities where people help each other are often stronger and more cohesive. This support network can be invaluable in times of need, such as during emergencies, natural disasters, or personal crises. For example, neighbors who help each other during a power outage, by sharing resources or checking on elderly residents, contribute to a sense of security and solidarity. This collective resilience is built on trust, cooperation, and mutual support, and it can make communities more adaptable and better able to withstand challenges. The knowledge that one is part of such a community can be incredibly reassuring and fulfilling, providing a sense of belonging and security.

Moreover, the satisfaction of helping a neighbor can have positive effects on mental and emotional well-being. Acts of kindness and generosity have been shown to release endorphins, the body's natural "feel-good" chemicals, which can reduce stress and promote a positive mood. This phenomenon, often referred to as the "helper's high," is a well-documented psychological effect that underscores the connection between altruism and well-being. Helping others can also provide a sense of accomplishment and self-worth, boosting self-esteem and confidence. For example, a person who helps an elderly neighbor with household tasks may feel a sense of pride and satisfaction from knowing they have made a positive difference in someone's life. This positive reinforcement can encourage further acts of kindness and contribute to a cycle of generosity and well-being.

In addition to the immediate benefits, helping a neighbor can also have long-term positive effects on social cohesion and community development. When people help each other, they build social capital, which refers to the networks of relationships and trust that enable communities to function effectively. Social capital is a critical component of healthy, thriving communities, as it facilitates cooperation, communication, and the sharing of resources. For example, a community where neighbors regularly help each other is likely to be more organized and effective in addressing common challenges, such as improving local amenities or advocating for policy changes. This social capital can also provide a foundation for broader social and civic engagement, as people who feel connected to their neighbors are more likely to participate in community activities and support collective initiatives.

Furthermore, helping a neighbor can be an important way of addressing social inequalities and promoting social justice. Acts of kindness and support can help to bridge gaps between different socioeconomic, cultural, or demographic groups, fostering greater understanding and solidarity. For example, helping a neighbor from a different cultural background with language translation or cultural integration can promote inclusivity and reduce barriers to participation in community life. Similarly, providing support to neighbors facing economic hardship, such as through food drives or financial assistance, can help to alleviate some of the challenges associated with poverty and inequality. By addressing these disparities at a local level, individuals can contribute to broader efforts to promote social justice and equity.

The satisfaction of helping a neighbor is also influenced by the reciprocal nature of these relationships. While the primary motivation for helping others is often altruistic, there is also a recognition that acts of kindness can lead to reciprocal benefits. This reciprocity is not necessarily immediate or direct; rather, it is part of a broader social contract where individuals support each other in times of need. This mutual support can create a sense of security and trust, knowing that help is available when needed. For example, a person who helps a neighbor with a home repair may not receive immediate repayment but may find that the neighbor is willing to help them in the future, whether through a different act of service or by providing moral support. This reciprocal exchange strengthens social bonds and reinforces the values of cooperation and mutual aid.

Chapter 39: The Joy of Personal Reflection

The joy of personal reflection is a profound and enriching experience that encompasses the process of introspection, self-examination, and contemplation of one's thoughts, feelings, and experiences. This introspective journey allows individuals to gain deeper insights into their inner world, fostering greater self-awareness, understanding, and personal growth. In a fast-paced world where external distractions are abundant, the act of pausing to reflect on one's life can be a transformative practice, offering a space for clarity, peace, and emotional well-being. Personal reflection involves examining one's values, beliefs, aspirations, and experiences, and it can be facilitated through various methods, such as journaling, meditation, or thoughtful conversation. The joy derived from personal reflection is multifaceted, stemming from the discoveries made about oneself, the resolutions gained, and the sense of inner harmony it can bring.

One of the primary joys of personal reflection is the opportunity it provides for self-discovery and self-awareness. Through reflective practices, individuals can explore their inner landscapes, uncovering aspects of themselves that may have been hidden or overlooked. This process often involves examining one's strengths, weaknesses, fears, and desires, as well as understanding the motivations behind one's actions and decisions. For example, reflecting on a recent interaction that felt unsettling can reveal underlying emotions or triggers, such as feelings of inadequacy or past experiences that influenced one's reaction. This awareness can lead to a deeper understanding of one's emotional patterns and behavioral tendencies, allowing for more intentional and mindful responses in the future. The joy of self-awareness lies in the clarity it brings, helping individuals to navigate their lives with greater purpose and confidence.

Another significant aspect of the joy of personal reflection is the insight it provides into one's values and beliefs. In the hustle and bustle of daily life, it can be easy to lose sight of what truly matters to us. Personal reflection offers a space to reconnect with core values and beliefs, which serve as guiding principles in our lives. For instance, reflecting on moments of fulfillment and satisfaction can help identify values such as compassion, creativity, or independence. Understanding these values allows individuals to align their actions and decisions with what is most important to them, leading to a more authentic and fulfilling life. This alignment can also provide a sense of direction and purpose, as individuals are better equipped to set goals and make choices that resonate with their deepest values.

The joy of personal reflection also encompasses the exploration of one's life purpose and aspirations. Many people find meaning and fulfillment in life by pursuing goals that are aligned with their passions and talents. However, identifying these aspirations often requires a period of reflection and introspection. By contemplating questions such as "What am I passionate about?" or "What impact do I want to have in the world?" individuals can uncover their true interests and desires. This process can lead to the discovery of new career paths, creative pursuits, or personal projects that bring joy and satisfaction. The sense of fulfillment that comes from pursuing one's aspirations is deeply connected to the joy of personal reflection, as it is through reflection that these aspirations are clarified and brought to the forefront.

Personal reflection also plays a crucial role in emotional regulation and well-being. By taking the time to reflect on one's emotions and experiences, individuals can process and make sense of their feelings, reducing stress and anxiety. For example, reflecting on a challenging situation can help identify the emotions involved and the reasons behind them, allowing for a more balanced and calm response. This process of emotional regulation is essential for maintaining mental health and well-being, as it helps individuals manage their emotions in healthy and constructive ways. Additionally, personal reflection can foster a sense of gratitude and contentment, as individuals reflect on positive experiences and the aspects of their lives for which they are thankful. This practice of gratitude can enhance overall happiness and satisfaction with life.

The joy of personal reflection is also tied to the ability to learn from past experiences. Reflection allows individuals to review their actions and decisions, considering what worked well and what could have been done differently. This learning process is invaluable for personal growth and development, as it provides insights into how to handle similar situations in the future. For example, reflecting on a project that did not go as planned can reveal areas for improvement, such as time management or communication skills. By learning from these experiences, individuals can make more informed and effective choices moving forward. The sense of progress and growth that comes from learning and applying new insights is a significant source of joy and satisfaction in the reflective process.

Moreover, personal reflection can enhance relationships and interpersonal skills. Reflecting on interactions with others can provide insights into one's communication style, conflict resolution strategies, and empathy levels. For instance, reflecting on a disagreement with a friend can reveal underlying issues or misunderstandings, as well as areas where one could improve in listening or expressing oneself. This awareness can lead to more meaningful and respectful interactions, fostering stronger and healthier relationships. The joy of improved relationships and deeper connections with others is a profound outcome of personal reflection, as it enriches one's social life and sense of belonging.

The practice of personal reflection can be facilitated through various methods, each offering unique benefits and insights. Journaling is one of the most common and accessible forms of reflection, allowing individuals to write down their thoughts, feelings, and experiences. This practice not only helps to clarify one's thoughts but also serves as a record of one's personal growth and development over time. Meditation is another powerful tool for reflection, providing a quiet space to focus inwardly and observe one's thoughts and emotions without judgment. Guided meditation or mindfulness practices can help individuals develop a deeper awareness of their inner world and cultivate a sense of presence and acceptance. Additionally, engaging in thoughtful conversations with trusted friends, mentors, or therapists can offer new perspectives and insights, enriching the reflective process.

The joy of personal reflection is also connected to the sense of peace and tranquility it can bring. In the midst of a busy and often chaotic world, taking time to reflect offers a moment of stillness and introspection. This pause allows individuals to step back from the external noise and focus on their inner experiences, providing a sense of grounding and clarity. This inner peace is not just a temporary respite but can have lasting effects on one's overall well-being. Regular reflection can help individuals develop a more mindful and centered approach to life, reducing stress and enhancing resilience. The joy of this inner calm and balance is a cherished aspect of personal reflection, offering a sanctuary of peace amidst the demands of everyday life.

Furthermore, personal reflection can foster a deeper connection to one's spiritual or philosophical beliefs. For many, reflection is a spiritual practice that involves contemplating life's deeper questions and mysteries. This can include reflecting on one's purpose, the nature of existence, or one's relationship with the divine. This spiritual dimension of reflection can provide a profound sense of meaning and connection, offering comfort and guidance in navigating life's challenges. Whether through prayer, meditation, or philosophical contemplation, the exploration of one's spiritual beliefs can be a source of deep joy and fulfillment, enriching one's inner life and providing a sense of direction and purpose.

In addition to its personal benefits, the practice of personal reflection can also have a positive impact on one's contributions to the broader community. Reflecting on one's values and aspirations can inspire individuals to take action in areas that are meaningful to them, whether through volunteer work, activism, or community involvement. This engagement not only contributes to the well-being of others but also reinforces one's sense of purpose and fulfillment. The joy of making a positive impact in the world is a powerful outcome of personal reflection, as it aligns one's actions with one's deepest values and beliefs. This sense of contribution and service is often accompanied by a feeling of gratitude and appreciation for the opportunity to make a difference.

Chapter 40: The Achievement of Meeting Goals

The achievement of meeting goals is a profoundly satisfying experience that embodies the culmination of effort, perseverance, planning, and sometimes overcoming significant obstacles. Achieving goals can take many forms, from personal ambitions like mastering a new skill or improving physical fitness, to professional milestones such as securing a promotion or completing a major project. The joy and sense of accomplishment that accompany the achievement of goals are not only rewarding in themselves but also contribute to building confidence, self-esteem, and motivation for future endeavors. The process of setting, working towards, and ultimately achieving goals is a complex and dynamic journey that encompasses various psychological, emotional, and practical elements.

At the core of the achievement of meeting goals is the concept of goal setting itself. Setting goals provides direction and purpose, guiding individuals towards specific outcomes and giving their efforts a clear focus. This process often begins with identifying what one wants to achieve, which can involve personal introspection, assessment of one's values, and consideration of one's desires and needs. Goals can be short-term or long-term, specific or broad, and they can encompass various aspects of life, including career, health, relationships, personal development, and more. For example, a short-term goal might be to finish a book by the end of the month, while a long-term goal could be to run a marathon within a year. The act of setting goals is itself a declaration of intent, a commitment to striving for something beyond the present state.

One of the most significant aspects of achieving goals is the sense of accomplishment it brings. This accomplishment is often accompanied by a deep sense of satisfaction and pride, as individuals recognize the efforts and dedication that have gone into reaching their objectives. The completion of a goal serves as a tangible marker of progress, validating the work and sacrifices made along the way. For instance, a student who graduates after years of studying and hard work feels a profound sense of achievement, knowing that they have reached an important milestone in their educational journey. This feeling of accomplishment is not just about the end result but also about the personal growth and development that occur throughout the process.

The achievement of meeting goals also reinforces a sense of self-efficacy, the belief in one's ability to influence events and outcomes in one's life. Self-efficacy is a critical component of motivation and resilience, as it empowers individuals to take on challenges and persist in the face of adversity. When individuals achieve their goals, they build confidence in their capabilities, which can positively impact other areas of their lives. For example, an individual who successfully loses weight through consistent exercise and healthy eating may feel more confident in their ability to tackle other challenges, such as pursuing a new career or learning a new language. This increased self-efficacy can lead to a virtuous cycle of setting and achieving new goals, further enhancing one's sense of competence and self-worth.

Another important element of the achievement of meeting goals is the development of discipline and perseverance. Achieving goals often requires sustained effort, patience, and the ability to overcome obstacles and setbacks. This process can be challenging, as it may involve stepping out of one's comfort zone, dealing with failures, and staying committed even when motivation wanes. However, these challenges are also opportunities for growth and learning. For instance, an entrepreneur who faces multiple rejections before securing funding for their business learns valuable lessons about resilience, adaptability, and persistence. The discipline and perseverance developed through the pursuit of goals are transferable skills that can benefit individuals in various aspects of their lives, from professional endeavors to personal relationships.

The journey towards achieving goals also involves careful planning and time management. Effective goal setting often requires breaking down larger objectives into smaller, manageable steps, setting deadlines, and creating a plan of action. This process helps individuals stay organized and focused, ensuring that they make steady progress towards their goals. For example, someone training for a marathon might create a running schedule, gradually increasing their mileage over time, while also incorporating strength training and rest days. By breaking the goal into smaller, actionable steps, the individual can track their progress and make adjustments as needed. This planning and time management not only facilitate the achievement of the goal but also help develop organizational and problem-solving skills.

Moreover, the achievement of meeting goals can lead to positive changes in one's habits and lifestyle. In the pursuit of goals, individuals often adopt new behaviors and routines that support their objectives. For example, someone aiming to improve their health may start incorporating regular exercise, healthy eating, and sufficient sleep into their daily routine. These new habits, developed in the context of goal achievement, can have long-lasting benefits, contributing to overall well-being and quality of life. The process of achieving goals can thus serve as a catalyst for positive change, helping individuals establish healthier and more productive habits.

The achievement of meeting goals is also closely linked to the experience of personal fulfillment and meaning. Goals often reflect an individual's values, passions, and aspirations, and achieving them can provide a deep sense of purpose and satisfaction. For instance, a person who sets a goal to volunteer regularly at a local charity may find fulfillment in knowing that they are making a positive impact on their community. This sense of purpose and meaning is a crucial component of well-being, as it contributes to a sense of belonging and connectedness to something greater than oneself. The joy of achieving meaningful goals is not only about the personal benefits but also about the contribution one makes to the well-being of others and society as a whole.

Additionally, the process of achieving goals often involves learning and skill development. Whether the goal is to learn a new language, acquire a professional certification, or develop a creative hobby, the pursuit of goals provides opportunities to expand one's knowledge and skills. This learning process can be deeply rewarding, as it enriches one's intellectual and creative capacities. For example, someone learning to play a musical instrument may experience the joy of mastering new techniques and pieces, while also developing patience, discipline, and creative expression. The acquisition of new skills and knowledge not only enhances one's capabilities but also opens up new possibilities and experiences, adding to the richness and diversity of life.

The social aspect of achieving goals is another important consideration. Many goals involve or impact others, whether it be collaborating with colleagues on a work project, participating in a team sport, or sharing personal achievements with family and friends. The support and encouragement from others can be a significant source of motivation and inspiration, helping individuals stay committed to their goals. Additionally, sharing the joy of achievement with others can strengthen relationships and foster a sense of community and connection. For example, celebrating a promotion or the completion of a marathon with loved ones can enhance the joy of the achievement, as it is shared and acknowledged by those who matter most.

Furthermore, the achievement of meeting goals can have a positive impact on one's mental and emotional well-being. The process of setting and working towards goals provides structure and purpose, which can be particularly beneficial during challenging or uncertain times. The sense of progress and accomplishment that comes from achieving goals can boost mood and reduce stress, providing a sense of control and agency. Additionally, achieving goals can enhance self-esteem and confidence, as individuals recognize their ability to set and accomplish meaningful objectives. This positive self-regard is an important aspect of mental health, contributing to a more optimistic and resilient outlook on life.

Epilogue

As we come to the end of "The Joy of Small Wins: Celebrating Daily Achievements," it's essential to reflect on the journey we've taken together. This book has been a celebration of the everyday moments that often pass by unnoticed but hold the power to bring immense joy and satisfaction.

Throughout these chapters, we've explored a diverse array of small wins, from the simplicity of a morning routine to the complexity of mastering a new skill. We've seen how small acts of kindness, personal achievements, and moments of mindfulness can create a tapestry of joy in our lives. By shifting our focus to these seemingly minor victories, we've uncovered the profound impact they have on our overall well-being and happiness.

The journey doesn't end here. The principles and practices discussed in this book are meant to be integrated into your daily life, transforming the way you perceive and celebrate your achievements. Every day presents a new opportunity to recognize and savor these moments. The key is to remain mindful, to appreciate the present, and to acknowledge that every small win contributes to a larger, more fulfilling picture.

As you continue on your path, remember that life is a collection of moments. While the big milestones are significant, it's the small, consistent victories that build the foundation for lasting happiness and success. Celebrate each step, no matter how small, and take pride in your journey.

Let this book be a constant reminder that joy is not just found in the destination but in every step along the way. Embrace the small wins, celebrate them wholeheartedly, and allow them to fuel your passion and drive. By doing so, you will cultivate a life rich with meaning, purpose, and joy.

Thank you for joining me on this journey. May your days be filled with countless small wins, each one bringing you closer to a life of profound joy and fulfillment.

The End.

www.ingramcontent.com/pod-product-compliance
Lightning Source LLC
Chambersburg PA
CBHW022003120726
47992CB00001B/394